£10

CW00348837

The Anthroposophical Understanding
of the Soul

The Anthroposophical Understanding of the Soul

by

F.W. Zeylmans v. Emmichoven

Anthroposophic Press
Spring Valley, New York

The original Dutch edition of this work bears the title
De Menselijke Ziel and was first published in 1946.
This volume was translated by Friedemann Schwarz-
kopf and received editorial attention from Charles
Davy, William La Tourette, Christopher Schaefer, and
Alice Wulsin.

Zeylmans van Emmichoven, F. W. (Frederik Willem),
1893–1961.
The anthroposophical understanding of the soul.

Translation of: De menselijke ziel.
Includes bibliographical references.
1. Soul. 2. Anthroposophy. I. Title.
BP596.S63Z4813 1982   299'.935   82-25283
ISBN 0-88010-019-2

Cover Design by Peter van Oordt

Printed in the United States of America

Table of Contents

Introduction

If we were to define how the understanding of the soul repre-
sented in this book is related to contemporary schools of
thought, there are three thinkers—Herder, Goethe, and
Steiner—whose spiritual outlook has had a decisive influence. The fact that none of these thinkers became particularly well known in this field is not so surprising if we take
into account the comprehensive wisdom and spiritual depth
which distinguish their works.

Herder's importance for a knowledge of the soul has
been pointed out by Krueger, who demonstrated how
Herder's profound insight penetrated the whole range of
soul-life with understanding, and in particular how Herder
was able to interpret in psychological terms the many-sided
development of the culture of his time. Krueger also showed
how Herder came "near to anticipating all the comparable
problems that emerged in subsequent cultural research."[1]
This was possible only because of his profound and thorough
consideration of spiritual events on their own account.
"With his passionate conviction that all living occurrences
in the realm of the spirit are determined by feelings, his
methodical questioning, his coherent presentiments concerning the evolutionary theory of culture, this deeply
thoughtful man is in the front rank of psychologists of his
century."[2]

Herder's way of thinking is characterized above all by
his feeling for the totality of things and for the relationships
and inner bonds between them. Nowadays many people like
to apply the word "romantic" to this way of thinking and to
contrast it with the "scientific" way. This is quite justified
if "scientific" is taken to apply only to thinking based on
perception, experiment, and intellectual deliberation. But
anyone who esteems ideas that spring from a profound wisdom, embracing humanity and the world, will recognize in

Herder not only a front-ranking scientific thinker but someone whose scientific method gains particular luster and
fervor through its intimate link with religion and the arts.

In his main work, *Ideas on the Philosophy of Human History*, Herder started from the relationships among the earth,
the individual, and mankind, and between all three and the
universe. The earth, as a "star among stars" and as "one of
the middle planets," is especially designed to enable man,
expressing in all his manifold forms the same archetype, to
achieve an evolution that makes him the crown of creation.
Herder saw not only the relationships between things and
appearances; he also recognized the long series of ascending
forces which, originating from an invisible world, become
visible in the forms that exist on earth. For him, evolution
meant "progress." Man stands at the end of a long series of
natural forms, but in so far as his spiritually emerging form
is concerned, he stands equally at the beginning of a new
series. He stands in the middle between the natural and the
divine world order.

Here is a fruitful starting-point for a psychology of the
soul that seeks to know man in a continual state of becoming,
growth, and development. Probably no one doubts Goethe's
practical knowledge of the human soul. To the psychology
of the soul he paid little heed, though certain aphorisms of
his in this field suggest the depth of his view. Lavater's
study of physiognomy interested Goethe mainly in connection with his own studies of the forms of plant, animal, and
man. It did not raise for him any special questions concerning the psychology of the soul.

Much more important for us is the way in which Goethe
treated the world of phenomena, notably in his scientific
works, the *Metamorphosis of Plants* and the *Theory of Colours*.
Just as with Herder, who had an important influence on the
shaping of Goethe's thought, the relationships between phenomena and their place in the world are the obvious starting-
point for Goethe. Man himself stands within these relation-

ships and is a part of this world, which he apprehends in a twofold way: through perception and through the forming of ideas, i.e., through "observation" and "intuition."[3]

In a letter from Schiller to Goethe, dated August 23, 1794, this method is excellently characterized: "Your observing gaze, which rests so calmly and purely on things, never brings you into the danger of going onto a side-track where speculation, as well as arbitrary, irresponsible fancy, can so easily lead one astray. Your true intuition embraces everything that is laboriously sought for by analysis, and goes beyond it." And later: "You take into account the whole of Nature in order to throw light on a single part; you search through the whole range of natural phenomena for an explanation of the individual. From simple organisms you rise step by step to more complicated ones, in order finally to build up genetically the most complicated of them all, man, with constituents drawn from the entire realm of Nature. By recreating him in accordance with Nature, so to speak, you seek to penetrate his hidden workings."

This "recreating" is the highest stage to which "living thinking," as we will call it from now on, is able to rise. The results of "pure observation" are the best preparation for it. This is the starting-point of any purely phenomenological method. In this respect, Goethe was without doubt one of the greatest phenomenologists of modern times. The way in which he let the phenomena speak to him and sought to understand their language, without allowing himself to be led astray by preconceived hypotheses, is exemplary. In the Preface to his *Theory of Colours*, he characterized his method in a few words: "If we set out to express the nature of a thing, it will be in vain. Effects are all that we can perceive, and a complete history of these effects would embrace the nature of the thing. Vainly we try to describe the character of a man; but if we bring together his actions, his deeds, then his character will emerge from them."

Perception and idea make a reality only in conjunction

with one another.[4] Through perception, appearances become mental images. The reality, the essence of being that expresses itself in these images, is not attainable in this way. We come into relationship with that reality only when the ideas, or "thought-pictures" (*denkbeelden*), are born into the soul through the living force of thinking. This thinking is universal, "beyond subject and object," as Steiner said, and can therefore connect a man with his "I." At the same time, this relationship is the most intimate link there can be between the cognitive activity of the soul and the universe. "Perceiving the idea in the reality is the true communion of man."[5]

The great importance of Goethe's polarity theory, especially for the psychology of the soul, will be referred to here on several occasions. Polarity, enhancement (*Steigerung*), and metamorphosis are three fundamental ideas indispensable to any psychology hoping to penetrate to the reality of the soul. Many psychologists of our time—Klages and his students among others—like to refer to Goethe and, in connection with him, to Carus. We will show presently that the way in which they apply Goethe's polarity theory is incorrect. Carus and Fortlage are among the more well-known Goetheanists. Carus has without doubt enriched the psychology of the soul with a number of important ideas. He lacks, however, the well-nigh infallible certainty of perception that we find in Goethe, and here and there he goes in for attractive but scarcely justified speculations. His noble-minded idealism and his deeply spiritual view of the relationship between man and the world nonetheless make him an important psychologist. Fortlage has already earned immortality with his theory of consciousness as a force of death. We will discuss its significance later.

Steiner's many-faceted lifework includes a number of books and lectures that deal with purely psychological matters. We shall follow his observations primarily. In his hands, Goethe's method was applied further, to the whole human being and his position between earth and universe. Thus Goethe's theory of metamorphosis provided for Steiner a solid foundation for an encompassing knowledge of man, culminating in his doctrine of threefold man. The human being, in his full manifestation as body, soul, and spirit, is central to all Steiner's considerations. Only by such means can we come to know the soul in its real essence.

For his own psychological observations, Steiner used the term "psychosophy," a term that had been used in that way at a much earlier date but had not endured.[6] Steiner's psychosophy begins with the deep interrelationships between phenomena that reveal themselves in the universe. Science thereby becomes wisdom, and only through such wisdom can the nature of the soul appear in its full light. Of the greatest importance also is the place Steiner assigned to the "I," or Ego, in relation to the body, the soul, and the spirit. According to him, the "I" is the kernel of the personality, and therefore what one finally "is." For the "I," "being" is a continual "becoming," the "I" that "always becomes but never is," as Steiner characterized it. The "I" is the most real thing in us and yet the hardest to grasp, even for an unusually subtle mode of psychological observation. We have a *picture* of the "I" in the human figure, an *experience* of it in the soul, and a *mental image* of it in our consciousness. But the reality of the "I" can be known only through further development of our capacity for knowing.

Since Külpe, the "I" has gained a place in more recent psychology. He no longer considers the soul as a mechanism but as a living and active whole, ruled and guided by the "I": "The 'I' sits on the throne and governs. He notices, perceives, and scrutinizes anything that enters his kingdom. He consults his experienced ministers, the basic principles and standards of his realm; he draws on his store of knowledge and insights; and he takes account of the needs of the moment and then decides on his attitude—whether to ignore the invading element, to make use of it, or to react against it."[7]

Through the utterance of this courageous thought, the soul as a reality was brought back into the realm of modern thinking. Now, however, soul and consciousness must be clearly distinguished. This point was elucidated by Steiner in his obituary essay on Brentano,[8] in which Steiner showed that anyone who takes the phenomena of consciousness for the real life of the soul makes the same mistake as one who, on seeing his figure in a mirror, believes that the mirror has brought his figure into being. Even though this mirror-image depends to a certain extent on the quality of the mirror, what it reveals has nothing to do with the mirror. "Human soul-life must have a picture of its own being if it is to fulfill itself within the sense-world. It must have this picture in its consciousness; otherwise it would indeed exist, but it would have no awareness of its existence. This picture, however, is entirely conditioned by the body's instruments. Without them it would not be there, just as the mirror-image would not be there without the mirror. The soul-life itself, however, reflected by the picture, depends no more in its own being on bodily instruments than the observer of his own mirror-image depends for his existence on the mirror. Only the soul's ordinary consciousness, not the soul itself, depends on bodily instruments."[9]

In this same essay Steiner also spoke about Brentano's interpretation of intentional relationships and the specific threefoldness that Brentano saw as the basis of soul-functions. Steiner's critical discussion of these views opens numerous new directions for modern psychology.

Recently, many of the thoughts advanced by Herder, Goethe, and Steiner have found their way into the psychology of the soul, although researchers who make use of them generally are not aware of their origin. The world of the spirit is all-embracing; during a given period, certain ideas are actively in vogue, but their source is not always recognized. It is a welcome insight, all the same, that the soul, as a living, developing unity, wherein the relationship between the "I" and the world is not only passively present in consciousness but is actively grasped and formulated, is no longer an unknown phenomenon in psychology.

Husserl's phenomenological method, Scheler's profound theory of the relationship between soul and spirit, along with *Gestalt*-psychology, open wide perspectives for a psychology of the soul that not only has theoretical significance but that can become fruitful in many practical areas of life.

I. The Nature of the Soul

HOW CAN ONE INVESTIGATE THE SOUL?

The Paradoxical Nature of the Soul

Anyone trying to write about the human soul will soon realize that it is full of secrets, difficult to conceive let alone understand. If we reflect on the nature of the soul, we may believe we are on the track of some essential feature, but when we try to capture it in words, we realize that a dead concept has replaced a living reality.

The mysterious entity we call "soul" has the most manifold and contradictory qualities. It is both omnipresent and scarcely discernable; it is widely open and firmly closed, as powerful as it is delicate. The soul can harbor eternal thoughts side by side with transient desires. If we really wish to know the soul, we must not hesitate to accept its paradoxical nature, full of contradictions as it is. We may even discover that precisely these paradoxical characteristics are an essential property of the soul.

The Use of Words in This Book

A description of the soul will require words and concepts adapted as much as possible to the nature of the soul itself. The development of modern natural science and of abstract philosophy has often led to chaos, because words and ideas, valid in these fields, have been applied all too often to the study of psychology. We shall therefore have to return as much as possible to the original meanings of words, drawing thankfully on everything in the use of language that has remained under the wise guidance of the spirit of language itself. The words of great poets and thinkers, too, will be of essential help. We must not hesitate to use these words in all their simplicity, even if this sometimes strikes a trained psychologist as naïve.

1

Direct and Indirect Perceptions of the Soul

In the inner peace of our being, the content of our soul-life reveals itself. Contemplation of this content gives rise to the need to reflect on it. By thinking, we put into order the manifold variety of phenomena. The content of our soul-life then reveals itself in forms, in pictures, which live as thoughts in the soul. Through such thoughts, ever more vast and profound relationships can be opened to us. By observing and thinking in this way, we step out of our own soul into the realm where we directly or indirectly meet the souls of our fellow men. We speak of direct or indirect meetings because, contrary to what is usually believed in psychology, direct observation of the soul of others is possible where a soul manifests itself through gesture, sound, tone, word, or thought. We speak of indirect observation if we must first interpret the outward behavior stemming from another soul. Anyone can make this distinction with a little good will. A man's gesture, for example, or the sound of his voice, can reveal directly a certain inner quality of his particular soul. In other cases, we can observe how the soul remains hidden behind its usual modes of behavior, especially when these are governed by social conventions and the like.

The thoughts that arise from observing our own souls and the souls of others are therefore increasingly able to bring before us the nature of the soul itself. The main laws concerning the soul's nature and development can be formulated in general terms, with a certain number of special cases added to complete the description.

Self-Perception of the Soul; "I"-Consciousness

Down through the centuries it has been recognized that the soul is able to perceive itself. Not only can the soul perceive the world, but it can perceive this perception, i.e., we are able to perceive that we are perceiving beings. We see a tree by means of our eyes, but neither the eye nor the optic nerve nor the brain sees the tree. When we say, "I see a tree," we are pointing to something in our complex being that is the real bearer of the perception.[10]

We can therefore assume that more happens in our soul than just the forming of percepts. We can, for example, perceive that we are in a good or a bad mood, that we are happy or sad, reflective or thoughtless, full of intent or lethargic. This inner perception has been recognized since the time of Plato and Aristotle. Aristotle especially discussed this question in his theory of the senses, or the capacity for sense-perception, and came to the conclusion that there exists no particular sense for this inner perception but that every sense must have the capacity to perceive itself. He thus directed attention to a common property underlying the wide variety of our sense-perceptions.

Modern psychology has brought this inner perception, or self-perception, into closer connection with the question of consciousness. For us, it is a direct expression of self-consciousness or "I"-consciousness, and the reason for this is a circumstance we will describe later: that the soul can come to a spiritual awakening in which the real kernel of the whole personality, the "I," lives and works. The same self-perception, rooted in this "I"-consciousness, enables us to make observations of the soul that are not bound up with our own soul-experience and yet that concern the soul as such. If we carefully and continually practice self-perception and relate it to the results of perceiving other souls, we shall garner a core of perceptions indispensable for thoughtful considerations in this field.

GENERAL CHARACTERISTICS OF THE SOUL

Inner Experiences; The Word "Soul"

It is generally recognized that in speaking of the human soul we are speaking of the inner life. It is perhaps even more accurate, however, to speak of an inner experiencing rather

3

than merely an inner life (*beleven* and *leven*). In the concept of experiencing, the active force of including, directing, or excluding is expressed. One can compare (in Dutch) this more active element of *be—leven* and *beleven*—with *treden* and *betreden*, walking and striding purposefully; *schouwen* and *beschouwen*, perceiving and actively looking; and so on. This inwardness also appears when we speak of the innermost part of an object. One can speak of the "soul" of a feather, of a song, and so on.

The origin of the word "soul" seems to be somewhat uncertain. The English "soul," Dutch *ziel*, and German *Seele* are connected with the Althochdeutsch *sela*, Middle Dutch *siele*, and Anglo-Saxon *Sawol*, and all these with the Gothic *saiwala*. One suspects originally a relationship with the Greek *saifolo*, so that the notion of mobility, even of impetuous movement, would be expressed. The earlier presumed connection with Dutch *zee* (sea), Old German *saiwitz*, sounds plausible but appears to be etymologically unjustified. In any case, the relationship in usage and tradition with mobility is evident, especially with mobility in the air. (The soul is often compared to a bird or a butterfly.) In other languages (compare *anima*, *atman*), the relationship with wind and breath is strongly expressed.

In the word "soul" (*ziel*, *Seele*), an inner area signified by the vowel is enclosed by the voiced or unvoiced "s" and "l." We will speak in greater detail in a later chapter about the significance of vowels and consonants. If one tries to let the sounds speak, one can experience something in the "l" that expresses an element of growth, of development or display, whereas the voiced or unvoiced "s" reflects much more a link with the bodily. Hence the word "soul" can be heard as a sound-picture in which an unfolding inwardness, linked with the bodily, is expressed.

The word "soul" is used also to characterize a man, i.e., a great soul, a poor soul. In earlier times, it was not uncommon to speak of a community made up of so many "souls."

The Involution of Qualities; The Development of Consciousness

We therefore describe the soul as an inner world, a world brought into being by involuting processes. The principle by which this involution was made possible we call the "kernel of the personality," or the "I." An involution was thus brought about around the "I" and even by the "I." As a result of this process, a part of the universe lives in a personal form within us; we carry a part of this universe personified within us. Everything that exists in the cosmos lives also—at least to a certain degree—within our soul. The things in the world exist within our soul in so far as they are not physical-material but spiritual and essential (of essence).

The elements of the universe that are involuted within our soul are qualities, spatial as well as temporal, sensory as well as moral. As Goethe speaks of the eye having been created "by the light for the light, so that the inner light may meet the outer light," so one could say of the soul that it has arisen "from the world for the world, in order that the inner world may meet the outer world," and that the soul may perceive the world and become conscious of it. "Were not the eye sunlike, how could we perceive the light? Lived not within us God's own force, how could the Divine enchant us?" Goethe expressed in these lines the ancient Greek idea that like can be perceived and known only by like. Regarding the soul one could ask: If the world were not living within our soul, how could we come to know the world? How could we experience, feel, perceive, and think over all that is present in the world?

If we are speaking here about an inner world, this is not meant in a spatial sense. We can, however, receive an image of this inwardness by watching the important role of involution in embryonic development, or by picturing the many

5

cavities in the body that depend on a process of involution in the organism. Comparative anatomy can teach us that the development of consciousness is connected with a further differentiation of this involuting process.

The inner world that we call "soul" cannot be fixed spatially, but we can learn much about it from the anatomical pictures we encounter in the world of animals and men. Consider, for example, the strange metamorphosis of the tadpole, in which the eyes come to protrude and movement by means of the limbs becomes possible at the very moment when the involuted lungs take over the breathing function from the gills. At the same time, the animal can express itself, in the sense that it can give voice to sounds by means of the air streaming from inside to outside. This connection is even more evident in the higher animals and in man. Out of the involuted cavity appears a qualitative element, the sound of the voice, which serves to make an inner impulse audible.

The Intentional Relationship to the World

If we conceive of the soul as an involuted world, which is in essence akin to the universe and lives in its qualities, the relationship between the soul and the world becomes clear: the activities of the soul are always linked with something in the world and always directed towards something in it. Every phenomenon of the soul is related to something in the world. Here one usually speaks of intentional relationships. This important notion is already found in Aristotle; it later reappears in the Scholastics, and again in modern psychology in Brentano:

> The common characteristic of everything psychic consists in something—often given the misleadingly

subjective name of consciousness—which has an intentional relationship to elements that are perhaps not really objective but yet are inwardly so. No hearing without something heard; no belief without something believed in; no hoping without something hoped for; no striving without something striven for; no joy without something to rejoice over, and so on.[11]

This characteristic of appearing always together with, or in relation to, something in the world, is indeed an essential property of the soul but is not peculiar to it. It proves that between soul and world exists an unbreakable link. It is not only psychic phenomena that are related to their surroundings, however; this applies also to physical phenomena, though in a different way. Steiner pointed out that Brentano's opinion—that between physical phenomena there are no intentional relationships—is incorrect.[12] Physical things, too, are inseparably linked in reciprocal relationships with their surroundings. Nothing in the world can be regarded as separate, existing for itself alone. The plant cannot be understood without bringing in earth, water, air, light, and warmth; even sun, moon, and stars are necessary for a complete picture.

In the same way, we cannot form a true concept of the soul without placing in the foreground its relationship to the universe. The fact of this relationship has to be established first, and the nature of the relationship must then be examined. In this context, Schuré's words, "L'âme est la clef de l'univers," "The soul is the key to the universe," gain a profound meaning. The soul makes the universe accessible to us, for the universe lives in the soul through its qualities. By this means the "I," which reveals itself to this inner universe, can enter into communication with the universe at large.

The Soul Participates in Two Worlds: the Physical-Corporeal World and the Spiritual-Moral World

In this inner world, which we call "soul," all sorts of different states and events appear. We usually distinguish perceptions and sensations, mental pictures and memories, feelings, desires, and drives, etc., without being concerned with the psychological meaning of these terms. Before we go on to describe all these phenomena, we had better consider how the soul itself should be characterized. We will begin by distinguishing various states and events and singling out from among them, on the one hand, certain facts that indicate a relationship between the soul and the surrounding world and, on the other hand, facts that point to a relationship with something within ourselves. This "something" rises from an interior world that extends its influence into our inner life while remaining itself as yet unknown. In other words, the soul as an inner world participates in two worlds: an external world and a world that for the present we shall call a still deeper, interior world. Both worlds come to expression in the soul, and the soul has relationships with them both.

For the present we shall call the exterior surrounding world a physical-corporeal world, in the sense that it is physically-corporeally formed. Man belongs to it with his physical-corporeal nature. This physical-corporeal world communicates with the soul through its sense-perceptible qualities: form, color, tone, and so on. The other world that communicates with the soul we shall call for the present a spiritual-moral world. It too reveals itself through its qualities, although these are of a different kind.

Just as the world is given to us externally in form, color, tone, and so on, so it is given to us inwardly in certain standards such as good and evil, truth and falsehood, beauty and ugliness, and so on. The fact that these standards are experienced and elaborated differently during diverse stages

8

of cultural development does not undermine the reality of their existence.

The Degree of Participation; Abnormalities

Nothing that we meet in the external world—stones, plants, animals, or other men—is in itself part of our soul-life. The soul takes account of external things or beings only in terms of the extent to which it experiences them or participates in their existence. This participation may be strong or weak. A fleeting impression can leave a clear memory and thereby show that the soul did not merely pass by the event. A dramatic event can shock the soul to such a degree that it cannot liberate itself from the event for months, sometimes even years. Generally speaking, the soul of a healthy human being will be interested in its surroundings, certainly more in some things than in others, but the interest is there, or at least capable of being aroused. We regard it as unhealthy or abnormal if this kind of participation is lacking, as, for example, in states of idiocy, schizophrenia, or melancholia. The other extreme, an excessive degree of interest, can also denote a sign of illness, if, for example, the soul cannot liberate itself from certain aspects of its surroundings, as can happen in states of obsession or anxiety.

Experiencing Truth, Goodness, and Beauty

Again, the thoughts and impulses that rise into the soul from the hidden world, called here a spiritual-moral world, are not in themselves part of our soul-life. The soul has the possibility of experiencing the truth about something. What then concerns the soul is not the truth as such but its own experience of it. The truth that $2 \times 2 = 4$ has not been calculated by the soul. For the soul, it is a given fact, given inwardly in the same way that stones, plants, and animals are given externally. Yet from such truths the soul experiences something: satisfaction or joy, or, in the case of an untruth, anger or pain. Hence the soul is not indifferent to whether something is true or untrue.

In addition to the experience of truth, there are moral experiences. Here again we can observe that the soul is not concerned with the fact of something being good or bad but with its own experience of any such issue and its own particular interest in it, which will vary from soul to soul. Something similar can be said about the experience of beauty. Here, too, we can regard as unhealthy or abnormal one who takes no interest in these three revelations of the spirit within us. Consider, for example, certain psychic states in which all sense of truth is lacking or in which there is no moral experience. The lack of any sense for beauty is also anomalous; however, this is not the same thing as the lack of a higher feeling for art.

The Soul as Mediator; The Level of Development

We therefore find the soul acting as mediator between two worlds: the outer world with all its phenomena, a given in relation to the soul, and the inner world, equally given, meet each other in the soul. The soul relates these to each other and finds its real being in continuously interweaving them to constitute the intrinsic realm of the soul. The outer world reveals itself to us by means of sense-perception. The senses can be seen as the gates of the soul, through which the qualities of the outer world stream in. These qualities can be seen, heard, touched, and so on, by the soul.

The inner world is not perceptible by the senses, but an inner capacity for perceiving is present within us. Our sense for truth, goodness, and beauty is as real as the visual sense for colors, the hearing sense for musical tones, etc. The fact that such an inner sense is not equally well developed in everyone is no argument against its existence. The ordinary senses, too, are very unequally developed in different people. Think, for example, of a painter's color sense or of a musician's ear for tone. In addition, a man is even more at

10

the beginning of his development regarding this inner sense than he is regarding his ordinary senses. As a spiritual-moral being he is far less developed than as a physical-corporeal being.

The Forming, Directing Influence of the Two Worlds

From both worlds something emanates that gives form and direction to the soul. The exterior world of sense-perceptible phenomena, and equally the interior world of spiritual phenomena, are given appearances. They *are*. The soul can, in the last analysis, only take account of the given. We can decide to go in a certain direction, but where a tree or a wall intervenes we must give way. Perhaps this is a crude example, yet it indicates that the whole sense-perceptible world surrounds us as a given situation of facts and conditions, and that the soul must take account of this. A great deal of the self-education of the little child, for example, consists in coming to know that the sense-perceptible world is given.

The inner spiritual world, too, shows itself to be given, and the soul cannot bypass it, even if seemingly one can ignore the forces working there. Anyone who does not wish to see a tree or a wall in his path will run against it and hurt his body. Anyone who refuses to recognize truth or morality will injure his soul. This inner world is also a source of active guidance and form-giving influence for the soul. It should be a task for education, especially of older children, to provide the right foundations in this realm.

The Polar Relationships of the Soul

This picture of the human soul as mediator between two worlds already shows us a certain polarity, which until now we expressed in the words: exterior and interior, outer and inner, physical-corporeal and spiritual-moral. These polarities are expressed to the highest degree in the relationships between soul and the worlds to which the soul is related.

In the spatial experience of the soul we distinguish up and down, front and rear, left and right; in the experience of time: before and after, earlier and later; in perception: light and dark, yellow and blue, bright and dim, major and minor, rough and smooth, sweet and sour; in emotion: pleasure and repugnance, joy and pain, tension and release, etc.; in moral values: good and evil, noble and mean; in the aesthetic realm: beautiful and ugly, harmonious and disharmonious; in science: true and untrue, correct and incorrect.

In the Preface to his *Theory of Colours*, Goethe described these relationships in the following words:

> We have a more and a less, an effecting, a resisting,
> an action, a passion, an advancing, a restraining,
> a vehement, a moderate, a male, a female, every-
> where notice and named; and so a language arises,
> a symbolism which can be used in similar cases as
> a parable, as a closely related expression, as a
> directly fitting word.

We shall have several opportunities later to show the significance of such a language, by which we can express the most important characteristics of the soul-life in a satisfying way.

The Relationship is Threefold: Body, Soul, Spirit

The soul's relationship to these polarities is that it stands always in the middle, between the poles. The polarities all originate in the soul through its relationship to the two worlds between which it finds itself. Something is experienced as being in front or behind, and in either of these relationships, or in both, the soul can participate. This holds good for all spatial, temporal, sensual, and other relationships.

We cannot understand the essence of these polarities, however, unless we keep clearly in mind that every polarity is an expression of a threefoldness, not of a twofoldness.

12

The third element, really the most important, is what lies between the two poles and through which the poles receive their true significance. Between the poles of an electromagnet is the current; between light and darkness are the colors; between the countless poles already mentioned lives the human soul.

In present-day writings on the psychology of the soul— e.g., those of Klages and his school—the term "polarity" is mostly used incorrectly, scarcely distinguished from "duality." The result is that the true meaning of polarity is lost; we are left merely with opposites, and how they communicate with each other remains an unanswered question. In Goethe's treatment of polarity, the essential nature of the object to be studied is made clear by the two poles between which it lies. Between light and darkness we meet the colors; the light itself is as invisible as the darkness; the colors are what we see. It is the same in Goethe's description of the metamorphosis of plants, in which the nature of the plant and its development can be understood only if we know the two fields to which the plant stands in polar relationship.

We will now describe in greater detail how the threefoldness with which we are here concerned is that of body, soul, and spirit.

The Soul in Continual Movement and Yet Constant

One result of this polar relationship is that everything in the soul is in continual movement, in the sense that we can think of soul-processes between two poles as a living stream. Since every movement takes time, we can speak of a continuous stream of events and processes. Hence the soul-life can be conceived only in dynamic terms. Outstanding among these movements in the soul is the one between the inner and the outer worlds, familiar in the regular rhythm of sleeping and waking. The soul is alternately withdrawn entirely into its own waking sphere or given over to the outer world. The same rhythm occurs during waking hours. If the

13

soul is given over to the enjoyment of nature or pays attention to the traffic, its attention is directed mainly outwards; when the soul is thinking something over or is living in a feeling of joy or pain, its attention is directed inwards.

Along with this element of continual movement, there is at the same time a certain constancy, i.e., although the soul moves from inside to outside, it never loses itself entirely either to exterior things or to its interior being. How this constancy is linked with the "I" that lives within the soul will be described later.

Horizontal and Vertical Movement;
Rhythm; Enhancement

Among these movements we can distinguish two main kinds, apart from those related to the polarities already mentioned. Movements of the first kind are associated with the relationship that the soul as an inner world has to its surroundings. This kind of movement is therefore directed from the interior outward or from the exterior inward. This kind of movement could be called horizontal. The second kind of movement is connected with an urge for expansion, for development, which is always present in the soul. This movement could be described as directed vertically.

The first kind of movement resembles the action of breathing: the soul lives alternately in outgoing and returning movements, like the breath that flows out and is drawn in again. Here we have to do with an alternating process of opening and closing, of getting in touch with the world and of isolating oneself inwardly. In connection with what we said earlier, we could also use here the image of an alternation between expansion and involution. The involuted world, which is our soul, opens itself to the surrounding world and then closes itself again.

A certain rhythm, such as is found in respiration, is also necessary here. If the soul directs its attention outwards for a long time, fatigue is the result, as during a visit to an exhibition. A moment of inner concentration can diminish this fatigue.

The experience of various polarities is closely related to this kind of movement, for example, the experience of light and dark, major and minor, sweet and sour, and so on. The soul expands in experiencing light, major, sweet, whereas it contracts inwardly in experiencing dark, minor, and sour.

The second kind of inner movement depends on the urge for display and development that lives in the soul. We will have more to say about this kind of urge later; for the moment, we can describe it as an urge of the soul to be consciously awake, in particular in relation to the two worlds between which it lives. We could also speak here of a movement in the sense of Goethe's "enhancement" (*Steigerung*).

The comparison with waking and sleeping is relevant here. In waking from sleep, the soul comes to consciousness that can gain in breadth and depth in the course of the day. Here too we find a certain rhythm. After being awake during the day, we feel a certain need for sleep; a period of inner enhancement raises the need to relax at a lower stage of consciousness, even if this need is only temporary. The movements mentioned here will be discussed in greater detail later.

The Soul in Space and Time; Dependent and Independent

The soul has a remarkable relationship to space and time. In a certain way it depends on these, but it is finally independent of them. We live constantly in an ever-changing pattern of spatial relationships. Our perception of all that exists in this spatial continuum is on the one hand restricted and on the other hand nearly unlimited. We see things in focus in our immediate neighborhood only to a certain extent, yet we see the stars, immeasurably distant, with the utmost clarity.

The same is true with regard to time. The soul is bound

to the immediate moment, yet past and future can be important for us at the same time. A percept or an inner experience may at a certain moment waken in us a memory-picture of something that happened years ago, or may call up an image of something that lies in the far future.

The words of the mystic, Angelus Silesius, come to mind:

> The soul has two eyes,
> One looks at time passing,
> The other sends forth its gaze
> Into eternity.

We could also characterize the relationship of the soul to time and space in the following way. The "here" and the "now" can both have a great, direct importance for the soul, but both can also be experienced as a single point, as one instant in the entire universe or in the eternal time-stream that connects past and future. The narrow boundaries of space and time in which the soul is caught by its bodily ties can be penetrated if another force works in the soul, the spiritual-moral force already mentioned.

The Urge toward Development

A further characteristic of the soul is its tendency to determine inner values. The soul lives independently of all conventions or religious dogmas, guided by its own urge to distinguish between good and evil, noble and mean, true and false. The wisdom of all the centuries speaks about this secret of the soul. We find it mentioned by the authors of the Vedas and the Upanishads, the Greek philosophers, the mystics, and by Goethe, whose words about the "two souls" have become almost common usage. We can also call it an innate urge for development, which has its origin in the nature of the soul itself.

It is impossible to describe a plant as a living being without showing that life is an essential part of it. Equally, one

16

cannot describe the human soul without showing this inner urge for development as one of its fundamental characteristics. This urge is found rooted in the hidden spiritual realm, the source of the three ideals to which the soul aspires: truth, beauty, and goodness. In every soul lives the desire to know something, to know more, to know what is right, and yes, finally, to know the truth. So it is with the urge to do good, to be good, to create something beautiful, and to experience beauty. These ideals are found in the most primitive societies and, on a higher level, in more advanced peoples. We find it in the little child as much as in the greatest philosopher.

The Need for Expression

This inner urge for development is united with the soul's need to express itself, to express what is born in the soul out of its relationships with the world. Expression comes about through movements formed in gesture, tone, sound, word, and thought. These modes of expression will be discussed in greater detail later.

We are concerned on the one hand with the inclination to perceive, to experience, that is, to bring the outer inward, and on the other hand with the inclination to give outward expression to the soul's inner life. These characteristics suffice to show that everything in the soul is related to various forms of movement: everything is in process, in continual development.

The Soul as Unity; Aberrations through Disturbances

The final, or, if you like, the first characteristic of the soul is that it is always active as a whole. The soul acts and reacts as one great, inwardly related unity. If we see or hear something, it is always the whole soul that participates in the process of hearing or seeing. If a feeling streams through us, be it joy or pain, it always fills us entirely. If we desire something, the whole soul is directed to its desire.

It may often seem different. Modern man especially is well acquainted with states of inner division, so-called schizoid states in which, for example, the soul cherishes a certain concept and yet an action is done that contradicts it. These states, however, are related to the fact that, owing to certain disturbances in the relationship between soul and body, forces are locked up in the soul, causing divisions that in serious cases give rise to illness. In the being of the soul as such no divisions of this kind can be found. In fact we find just the opposite: the soul's inclination always to be active as a unity. For example, if a particular sense-organ fails, the soul will unite itself all the more strongly with another sense-organ. So it is that blind persons often have a more sensitive musical ear or a subtler sense of touch than most sighted persons. Further evidence on this point comes from cases where the senses work together in a different way, for example, in the occasional phenomenon of color-hearing (*audition colorée*).

Here we must mention the remarkable fact that the various forces in the soul always function together in a certain sense. Feeling is always accompanied by forming mental images and by willing, and acts of willing by forming mental images and feeling. These phenomena all indicate that the soul is ultimately a single, related whole. Beyond doubt the reason for this is that the soul has as its center the spiritual-moral kernel of the personality, which we have called the "I," or Ego.

A Summary of Soul Characteristics

We can now describe the soul in the following summary:

1. As an *interior*, involuted world that contains within itself all the qualities that reveal themselves in the universe;

18

2. As *participant in the two worlds*: a physical-corporeal world, experienced by the soul as external, and a spiritual-moral world, experienced by the soul as internal;
3. As a *mediator* between these two worlds;
4. As being in a *polar relationship* with everything with which it connects itself;
5. As being *continuously in movement* between the various poles and yet inwardly *consistent* (invariable);
6. As thereby *living in a spatial and temporal relationship without being bound* to it;
7. As being *filled with an urge for development*, in connection both with the standards of the physical-corporeal world and with those of the spiritual-moral world;
8. As being equally able to *introvert the external* and to *give outward expression to its inner life*;
9. Finally, as a *unity*, acting and suffering (acting and reacting) as a whole.

The Place of the Soul; Contradictions in the Soul

Man thus experiences in his soul on the one hand his relationship to the surrounding world, in which we must take account of the human body and its organic processes, and on the other hand his relationship to an inner world, living deeply within him, which comes to expression in the soul and thereby reveals something of the real origin of the human being. In this relationship between the sense-world and the inner world, the soul develops itself. Novalis expressed this in the words: "The seat of the soul is where inner and outer world touch each other; where they permeate each other, it is in every point a touching."[13]

The great contradictions found in every human soul can be explained in this connection. The same soul can be noble and ignoble, powerful and powerless, broad and narrow, striving for the highest and capable of the lowest.

19

THE SOUL BETWEEN BODY AND SPIRIT

The Relationship between Body and Spirit

Nothing in the world known to us exists on its own account, i.e., quite unrelated to its surroundings. Nothing is conceivable as an isolated entity. We grasp phenomena through their relationships with other phenomena. The plant has its roots in the earth, lives in a stream of liquid, breathes in the air, and unfolds in light and warmth. Earth, liquid, light, and warmth are all necessary for understanding the being of the plant. We cannot understand the soul either without taking into account the relationships it has with its whole surroundings, in particular its relationship with body and spirit. Thus far we have described the soul as living between two worlds, a physical-corporeal world and a spiritual-moral world. In the human being, these two worlds are found in a personified form as body and spirit. In this sense we can say that man consists of body, soul, and spirit. Through his body he is part of the physical-corporeal world around him; as a spiritual being he is linked to the spiritual-moral world order, the foundation of all existence. The soul lives in its own inner world, which stands between the other two worlds and is related to both of them. It is open to both, without forfeiting its own being.

The Physical Body and the Life-Body

By "body" we understand here the whole system of forces with which man as a natural being takes his place in nature. Through our senses we perceive the body in the same way that we perceive surrounding nature with its three kingdoms. In so far as man is made of mineral substance and obeys the mechanical, physical, and chemical laws prevailing in the mineral world, he can be compared with the minerals. A truly "mineral state" of the body occurs only when the body dies, however. The corpse, left to itself, starts

20

to decompose and is received by the forces that work in inorganic nature.

This is not the case during life. A characteristic of living organisms is that they continually *overcome* these forces. The plant grows and unfolds in a direction away from the earth. Gravity is countered in a certain sense by the growth-process. The mineral substances that take part in the process of nourishment to a great extent lose their physical and chemical qualities and are transformed into living substance. Phenomena such as growth, the development of form and structure, propagation, and the like, which are characteristic of living organisms, cannot be explained by the laws of inorganic nature. The attempt to explain them in this way could arise only in an extremely materialistic period. In reality we must associate all living phenomena with a system of forces opposed, both in kind and direction, to the system of forces in which mechanical, physical, and chemical activities are found.

Steiner distinguished these two complexes of forces as earthly and cosmic, or as centripetal and centrifugal, and also as central and peripheral in so far as their direction is concerned. The law of gravity expresses the link of all mineral forms to the surface of the earth or, more accurately, to the center of the earth. The forces that govern living activities point to the opposite direction. They originate in the surroundings of the earth, namely in the universe, which appears to us as a sphere. They stream out of the cosmos into the living organism and continually withdraw it from the effect of the earthly forces. Steiner expressed this by saying that a living organism must cease to be regarded as "a mere part of the earth. It emancipates itself from its attachment to the earth. It is permeated by the forces which radiate onto the earth from all sides."[14]

This peripheral or cosmic complex of forces permeates, regulates, and dominates every living being. It is as fully formed as is the earthly complex of forces that is the basis of every mineral. We can therefore think of it as a "body": in the terminology of spiritual science, as a "body of formative forces," "life-body," or, following an older tradition, "etheric body."

For a long time modern natural science has acknowledged the existence of such a closed, inwardly coherent unity of life-forces but has been unable to find a method leading to the inner observation of their nature.

The Words "Body" (Lichaam) and "Life" (Leven); Life-Body and Plant Kingdom

We drew a distinction between the corpse, which is entirely visible only in death, and the living body, within which the forces of the mineral world are continually overcome by the forces of life. The Dutch word *lichaam* expresses the association with the term "dead body," the German *Leichnam*. This derives from the Anglo-Saxon *lic*, or Gothic *leik*, which means flesh, and the Anglo-Saxon *hama*, or Gothic *hamon*, which means "clothing" or "envelopment." Later, *lik* or *leik* acquired the meaning, *Leiche* (corpse). The word *Leib* (body) points more to the living body. It is related to the English "life," and derives from the Anglo-Saxon *lif* and the Althochdeutsch *lib*. In German usages, such as *Leiberserhaltung*, we find expressed a relationship with the life-processes streaming through the body.

By the life-body we mean the whole system of forces manifest in ever-changing forms in the organic processes of growth, nourishment and metabolism, propagation, and development. In so far as these processes function in him, man is related to the plant world. With the animal world the human being has in common the capacity to receive impressions from outside and to respond to them from within himself, to express his relationship to these impressions from within. Here we enter the realm of the soul.

This kind of response does not occur in the plants. In-

22

deed, they react to certain stimulations but without being able to experience them and to work upon them, and that is just what is essential. Iron also reacts to warmth by expanding, but we can hardly call this the expression of a soul. Only where an inner experience occurs and gives rise to some form of expression can we speak of "ensoulment."

The Soul-Body and the Animal Kingdom

In animals, these expressions of the soul are very limited, because they are strongly linked to the body and its life-processes. In connection with soul-expressions, we can also speak of a whole that shows itself always in a particular formation (*gevormdheid*). Here again, we speak of a "body," and, in harmony with spiritual science, of a "soul-body," because the forces that govern it transcend the cosmic forces mentioned above. They are the forces that, as Steiner puts it, make the earth itself into a "world-body," a "star" (*astrum*).[15]

Through physical forces the earth separates itself from the universe; through its life-forces or etheric forces it is related to the universe and is subject to its creative activity; only through the soul-forces—or "astral forces"—does it become an independent whole in the universe. In animals and in man these forces work in an inwardly enclosed form. To the extent that man has this soul-body within him he is comparable to the animal. Animals and human beings receive and assimilate impressions from their surroundings and then express outwardly what they have inwardly experienced. This is as far as animals can go, but for man it is only the foundation for his true path of development.

The Spirit; Pure Thinking, Feeling, and Willing

The real being of man springs from the spirit. Man has the corpse in common with the minerals, the life-body with the plant, the soul-body with the animal. The spirit and its

23

personal expression through the "I" belong to man alone. Through the spirit it is possible for us to know the enduring element in all phenomena: their essence, their significance, and their place in the universe. Through the spirit we raise ourselves above the sentiments and sensations that come and go in the soul, and we can thus find a calm spot within ourselves. The eternal in the world and in our existence reveals itself through the spirit.

The human spirit can discover the laws of lifeless and of living nature and the laws whereby things come into being and pass away. It also has access to the laws that can be discerned in the manifestations of beauty and to the laws that are the foundation of morality in the universe and in human life. Hence the spirit relates us to truth, beauty, and goodness, the three ideals that fill our soul. All that we can learn about these ideals through the soul's experience is the fact of their existence and our longing to reach them, which the soul cannot do on its own. Only in so far as the spirit liberates the soul entirely from its bodily bonds can the soul unite itself fully with these ideals. We have an inner impulse for truth, beauty, and goodness, but at the same time we understand that the soul as such can only strive for these three ideals without entirely reaching them. Only when the spirit has liberated the soul entirely of its bodily link can it fully unite itself with these ideals.

Through forming mental images we can make for ourselves a picture of the world but a picture that will change whenever we come to see that its truth is only relative. Only "pure thinking," i.e., thinking born out of the spirit, unites us with the truth. Similarly, willing can become "pure willing" through the spirit and thereby attain to the moral foundation of the universe. Between pure thinking and pure willing is "pure feeling," which is an inward connection between these two primal powers of the spirit. We could also speak here about thinking, feeling, and willing "as such," or of the thinking, feeling, and willing that spring from the spirit. The word "pure" denotes only this latter aspect.

Our relationship to things and phenomena in the world depends at first on our inner experience of them, and this is determined by sensations, feelings, and desires. Only through the spirit can this relationship, generally called subjective, become objective, i.e., a relationship in which things and phenomena reveal their true nature. In reality, however, our spiritual relationship to the world goes beyond the antithesis of subjective and objective, because this antithesis is created only through pure thinking and therefore by the spirit within us.[16]

The Difference between Man and Animal

Scheler excellently characterized the antithesis between animal and man by pointing out that man as a spiritual being has an open relationship to the world, while the animal is always ruled by its surroundings. The animal's inner link with the world comes about through sense-impressions and the urges connected with them:

> Anything not relevant to these urges is not there for the animal—he pays no attention to it. And anything that gains his attention serves only to activate his desire or his disgust.[17]

The animal knows no other world than that to which he is bound by his natural species. In reality he has no relationship to the world as such but only to his immediate environment. Scheler indicated this briefly but brilliantly with the formula $A \rightleftarrows E$ (animal $\rightleftarrows$ environment).

In a being endowed with spirit, a different relationship to the world is possible. An urge that is under control can be withheld or released by a free decision from the center of one's being. In brief:

$$M \rightleftarrows W \rightarrow\rightarrow (Man \rightleftarrows World \rightarrow\rightarrow)$$

For man it is not only his surroundings that are significant but the world. His world widens and he is able to examine it in ever-greater detail, depending on the extent of his spiritual development. The animal, by contrast, can never make its environment into a "world."

Elsewhere Scheler distinguished the human being from the animal as the being who *can* regulate his own life, which flows through him so powerfully, by restraining and repressing his urges and refusing to feed them with percepts and mental images. Compared with the animal, who always says yes to actuality even when it repels him, man is a nay-sayer, life's ascetic, the eternal Protestant opposed to all mere actuality.

Body, Soul, and Spirit as Appearance;
The Transitional Area Between Body and Soul

We began our considerations of the human soul with the threefoldness of body, soul, and spirit, in which is revealed the whole human being. In each case we are concerned with a certain form in which the reality of the human being finds expression. In this threefoldness we regard the body in the sense of the "living body." Hence we do not include the phenomena of life in the realm of the soul, unlike many modern psychologists (among others, Driesch) who more or less equate life with the soul. When Aristotle discusses the soul as starting from the realm of life and therefore recognizes a soul in the plant, we need raise no objection, for besides the nourishing or vegetative soul, which is identical with the "body of formative forces" or life-body, as we have described it, he is aware of various other "souls," such as the desiring soul and the thinking soul.

The equation of life with soul must be judged quite differently if it leads to seeing both as a unity, so that all life-phenomena must be explained in terms of the soul, or all soul-phenomena in terms of life. In that case we must reject the equation, for it would necessarily leave us with an impoverished range of mental images.

The soul is an inwardly coherent unity, as we have already pointed out. A careful examination of the laws governing the soul leads to the insight that the soul has a polar arrangement within itself whereby its place between body and spirit, and its relationship to them both, becomes evident.

The corpse, i.e., the dead body, is outside the realm of the soul. The living body, however, has forces that directly touch the complex forces of the soul and enter into relationship with them. Hence we can regard the life as a transition-area between body and soul. A similar transition-area lies between soul and spirit, and we shall come to this when we discuss the cognitive functions of the soul, for they are directly related to the activity of the spirit in the soul.

No Dualism; The Spirit as the Origin of All;
The Hierarchical Nature of the World-Order

It hardly needs to be mentioned that this approach leaves no place for dualism. Body and soul both have a spiritual origin. Everything that exists, in particular the human being, is born out of the spirit, rooted in the spirit, living and dying in the spirit. The spiritual unity that is the basis of the whole creation can be approached only in this way and thought of only in these terms. We cannot agree with the dualism still prevailing here and there in psychology. Lindworsky, for example, treats the soul as a being of spiritual origin, indeed as one that arose directly from divine creation, while he regards the body, by contrast, as material.[18]

We will have occasion to show later that a true conception of the body and the life-processes is possible only on the ground of these deep relationships between body, soul, and spirit. At the same time we must consider the spirit not only as the beginning of everything but realize that it is also the enduring foundation of all things, and notably of all phenomena connected with body and soul. Where else but in the spirit could we find the forces that build and form the body? Where else the forces that give rise to ordered thinking in the midst of manifold images, and to the noble feelings and will-impulses striving towards higher things, which emerge from the confusion of emotional impulses and instinctive drives?

That the body has definite forms and contours means that the activity of the spirit is more visible, tangible, and perceptible in general. To the life-processes flowing through the organs and organ-systems, the only path of approach is at first through thoughtful observation. The inner experience of the soul brings us into touch with the spirit in a more intimate way, but this has only a personal or so-called subjective significance. A relationship with the spirit that goes beyond the personal can occur only in those realms of the soul liberated from the bodily bonds by the activity of the spirit, so that now the spirit can awaken in the spiritual world-order.

Differentiation of the threefold nature of man is indispensable for a modern psychology of the soul. We are not dealing merely with a question of terminology, as Mannoury once said in a lecture,[19] but with the much more important question of distinguishing the actual stages whereby "being" manifests itself: in brief, with the question of the hierarchical order of creation. Only a way of thinking trained to encompass the deeply searching and yet comprehensive viewpoints of Herder, Goethe, and Steiner can offer true insight here. Essentially this is a way of thinking that acknowledges and understands the place of hierarchy in the world-order. In all the ancient wisdom-teachings, the hierarchical structure of the cosmos was recognized, as it was in early Christianity.

When Herder tried in modern times to define the position of man in relation to the three kingdoms of nature below him, he also had in view a "higher species of creatures," of which man is the lowest member.[20] In this hierarchical world-order, accordingly, man stands in the middle. Leibniz's expression that "the soul is a mirror of the universe" perhaps contains a deeper truth than that usually derived from it. The forces of the universe seem to be hidden in the soul, and the soul needs only an organization, or a chain of organizations, to enter into activity and practice.

Again, Goethe's contemplation of the whole process of "becoming" in nature is based on the notion of an ascending metamorphosis, a development as if on a spiritual ladder. Steiner carried this idea of development further. He took the names that had come down from the old hierarchical world-order, but that had lost their content, and endowed them once more with a deeper meaning. This is something that the psychology of the soul will have to take into account if it is really to progress.

The "I" as the Essence of the Personality

What finally expresses itself in our soul as the spiritual kernel of our personality, of our real threefoldness, we call the "I," or Ego. This "self-expression" has to be taken literally, for in every human being the moment comes when he feels himself to be a personal, independent being, distinct from all other beings in the world. This moment comes in childhood, when the child utters for the first time the little word, "I." Jean Paul described this as an event that takes place in a human being's most hidden sanctuary. It generally happens in the third year of life. Before this, a child is unable to distinguish himself consciously from his surroundings. He will call himself by a name he has heard others call him, just as he imitates the names of other people and things. It is only when the spiritual kernel of his personality penetrates into a child's consciousness, causing the first ray of spiritual consciousness to illuminate his soul,

29

that he experiences himself as an inner personality, as an "I-being." Steiner repeatedly emphasized that the little word "I" is a name that stands apart from all other names. Everyone, he said, can call a table a table, or a chair a chair; but "I" can be used only by the person concerned to designate himself.

The birth of the "I" in the soul, beginning around the third year, takes place step by step in various phases. Nearly everyone will remember, either from his own youth or from his later life, moments when he experienced himself as an "I," alone in relation to the world. These moments can be of great significance to the soul, for they are like milestones in the process of development. When the separation of the "I" from everything belonging to the world is experienced in the soul with all clarity and force, duality of "I" and "world" comes to full consciousness.

Formerly the word "I" was a collective name covering everything that appertained to the body and the soul. In ordinary usage this is still the case. Thus we say "I hurt myself," as readily as "I think," or "I will." At the moments mentioned above, however, when the "I"-experience is deepened and intensified, the difference between body and soul on the one hand and the "I" on the other hand stands out clearly. We then learn to know the "I" as the innermost force within us: a force that goes far beyond body and soul and, through its spiritual origin, that can work at forming and regulating both. Body and soul are finally placed in the service of the "I," in the sense that both become essential areas of experience in which the "I" can move. The sense-experiences that would not be possible without the body, the sensations and emotions, the feelings and desires that emerge in the soul, enable the "I" to recognize the tasks that are given to it. On the other side, the "I" opens and unfolds itself to the world of the spirit and finds there the appropriate directions for its activity.

The "I" is thus connected with everything in man, but

30

it cannot be equated entirely with anything. It is the eternal entelechy, the basis of our real being, the divine seed working in everything, permeating, forming, and transforming everything, finally ruling over everything as the personified divine spirit within us, which *was* before birth, *is* during life, and *will be* after death.

The Development of the Soul through the "I"

Only through the activity of the "I" is the human soul given its proper form. In the case of the animal we speak of a soul-body, and thereby of a system of forces equipped with soul-qualities. In man this system of forces becomes an inwardly formed whole showing a certain independence, whereas the soul-body of the animal functions only in connection with the surrounding world. Just as the human figure, with the "I" as its ruler, is quite different in kind from the animal-body, so is the human soul different in kind from the animal soul-body. In the human soul, the "I" is present as a working principle.

Our sensations, feelings, and desires, all our soul-forces, are connected with one another inwardly, and this depends not only on the world, but also—and even primarily—on the "I." Because of this, a continuous development of the soul takes place. Sensations and mental images are ordered, feelings are deepened and harmonized, and desires are directed and refined. In this way an inner balance evolves, the ground for thoughts that arise from the spirit, for moral impulses, and for loving feelings. One can thus speak of a development in the sense of a refinement, a clarification, and finally a spiritualization of the soul by the "I."

II. The Forces at Work in the Soul

FEELING AND JUDGING

Pleasure–Displeasure; Sympathy–Antipathy;
The World of Feeling

If we take as the starting-point for our further observations the description of the soul summarized on pp. 18–19, it will be clear that the soul's outstanding characteristic is its ability to participate in the two worlds between which it is placed. The soul can participate in various ways in the polarity already described, in the spatial or temporal realm, for example, as well as in the spiritual or moral. As far as this participation is concerned, however, we must distinguish between the two ways in which the soul behaves. We can speak of participation not only when the soul opens itself gladly to something agreeable, as when a baby drinks its mother's milk or a child tastes a sweet, but also when the soul withdraws in dislike from something unpleasant, as when a child tastes something harsh or bitter.

These two kinds of participation can be distinguished in every field. We can speak of an opening or a closing of the soul, an expansion or a contraction. The soul opens itself to a phenomenon if it is experienced as pleasant, beneficial, or comfortable. In the opposite case, if it is experienced as unpleasant, hostile, or uncomfortable, the soul tries to close itself as much as it can. We can also describe these two ways of behaving as the soul's movement towards a certain phenomenon or a turning away from it, as an affirmative or negative attitude of the soul. In its affirmative movements and attitudes, the soul experiences a positive feeling, a feeling of pleasure or of sympathy. In the opposite case, the soul experiences a negative feeling, a feeling of displeasure

32

or antipathy. Brentano[21] and Steiner[22] called this the "phenomenon of love and hatred."

We will call this experience of positive and negative "the experience of feelings" or, briefly, "feeling." This feeling has the same relation to "pure feeling" (already mentioned and to be described in more detail later) as associative thinking, in which existing mental images are connected in an associative way, has to "pure thinking," or as desiring has to "pure willing."

This feeling can, of course, move in all the polarities we have mentioned. It expresses something about the immediate situation of the soul, which either unites and merges with a phenomenon or withdraws and closes inwardly. In experiencing harmony, the soul opens itself and expands in the sounds; in experiencing disharmony, the soul closes itself and withdraws. When a warm feeling comes towards the soul, the soul feels a need to expand inwardly and to merge with this feeling, whereas in face of a cold feeling the soul is driven back within its own boundaries.

The Word "Feeling"; Positive and Negative
Feelings; Enrichment and Impoverishment of the Soul

The word "feel" must originally have had the meaning of "touch." The Indo-German root is *(s)p(h)el* or *(s)p(h)al* (Latin *palpo* = I caress, I stroke; Greek *pselaphao* = I touch). In the German, this developed from *phal (phel)* to *fal* or *fol*, the basis of *fühlen* (German) or *voelen* (Dutch). It is interesting to note the connections between *phal* and the word *palm* in Dutch and English. In psychological terms, therefore, feeling means to touch inwardly. The double direction which this process of touching can take is sufficiently clear. In one case, the touching becomes a gesture directed outwards; in the other, a withdrawal, or even a gesture directed inwards. In both cases we have to do with touching and the inner experience directly connected with it.

33

How can we identify the feeling of pleasure and joy that arises when, for example, the soul opens itself to a phenomenon and touches it? At the beginning of our observations we mentioned the close link between soul and world. Soul and world belong together; they are of the same kind, the same origin, and finally the same substance. The primal elements out of which the universe is made, the component parts of all being (including the human being), reveal themselves to the soul through their characteristics or qualities. The soul can participate in this revelation by opening itself to these qualities and touching them inwardly. Through this touching, a conjunction or a merging comes about, for in this realm there are no external dividing walls. This conjunction or merging of the soul with the most essential qualities of the universe gives the soul an immediate feeling of pleasure and joy, because it brings about a partial liberation of the soul. By expanding in these qualities, the soul moves out of the boundaries imposed on it by the body. It unites with the universe out of which it came at birth and again experiences something of the complete surrender to the breadth and the light that filled it during its prenatal existence.

In the opposite case, the soul is forced back into its own realm. The inner boundaries—those between soul and body —are removed. The soul feels linked more than ever to the outer world and experiences the imprisonment in the body. The soul resists the invasion of such qualities, by which it feels its existence to be disturbed, threatened, or injured, but it can do this only by closing itself and withdrawing within the boundaries of the bodily connection. Hence the soul feels lonely.

We can therefore describe the opposition between positive and negative feelings also as an opposition between the enrichment of the soul through union with the universe and an impoverishment through withdrawal from the universe: a feeling of relationship in one case, of loneliness in the other. In all portions of the soul, an essentially similar process takes place. Whether we are dealing with an experience in the realm of the senses, a superficial emotion, or a deep feeling, the opposition described always appears. This is demonstrated in language, in which the same words are often used for entirely different experiences. We speak, for example, of a sweet or a bitter taste as well as of a sweet joy or a bitter pain.

The Desire of the Human Soul to be One with the World Soul; Laughing and Weeping

From the preceding considerations, it follows that the experience of feelings originates in the desire of the soul to unite with the universe. If we take the emotional qualities of the universe as a manifestation of something we will call "world soul," our experience of feelings is an ever-changing relationship between human soul and world soul. In positive feelings a union occurs; in negative feelings, a separation. In positive feelings the soul is drawn out into the world; negative feelings draw it back to its own isolated existence. In the first case, the soul experiences a relationship with its spiritual homeland; in the second case, the loneliness of its earthly existence.

We can thus determine the nature of pleasure and joy. The soul finds itself in something of a paradisal connection with the most essential manifestation of all that exists. One's essential picture of the world changes; everything is warm, light, brilliant. The boundaries of space and time are broken. The soul is wide open and all-embracing. In our experience of repugnance and suffering, however, we experience the reality of the "lost paradise." The soul is chained to the earth. The surrounding world becomes cold and dark.

In every man's soul there lives a longing for positive feelings rising beyond the temporal and transitory, a longing for the pleasure that seeks the eternal. "Every pleasure craves

35

for eternity, deep, deep eternity," as Nietzsche said. By contrast, because of the polar relationships in which it lives, the soul repeatedly and painfully experiences its bondage to the temporal and other limitations of earthly existence. The soul of the newborn infant, who is just losing his relationship with the cosmos, gives vent in plaintive crying to this feeling of imprisonment in the body. At first the infant does little but sleep and drink, re-establishing in both the cosmic relationship. While sleeping he withdraws entirely from earthly life; while drinking he satisfies himself fully with the warm, sweet taste. Having drunk his fill, he falls asleep again or looks around, rosy and healthy, until hunger or some other discomfort reminds him of his exile and he starts to cry again. Usually he laughs for the first time when he is caressed or sees a laughing face turned toward him.

Laughing and weeping are the two inward movements of the soul that make visible the opposite poles of feeling. The laughing face relaxes, becomes round, and its lines point upwards; the weeping face is drawn, acquires harder and deeper lines, and its lines point downwards. In older children and adults, the opposite poles are no longer so clearly visible, but inwardly we find the same rhythmical movements of the human soul in relation to the world soul, alternating between union and separation.

Judgment as the Consequence of Separating, Negative Feelings

When the soul opens itself, it is permeated by the qualities that the world reveals, and it unites with them. If it closes itself, the soul becomes an independent part of the world and therefore stands in opposition to it. The soul itself is now a sum of the qualities, and it experiences this fact not *in* the world but free from it.

Can one regard negative feeling, which leads to independence, as being only negative? Does it express only a severance of relationship with the universe, or does it also have a positive aspect? In the experience of negative feeling, the soul has indeed disengaged itself from the universe, but thereby another relationship becomes possible: the world outside oneself can be experienced. We then find that its qualities can be experienced not only through feeling but also through *knowing*: knowing the world and even re-"cognizing" it. Since we carry all qualities within us in our soul, knowing the world is at the same time an inward act of recognition.

The word "judgment" (*oordeel*) here denotes the form in which the process of knowing and recognizing the world enters our consciousness. We do not mean here the complex process of forming judgments that will be described later, but solely the relationship between soul and universe characterized by knowing and recognizing its qualities. Feeling and judging are therefore directly related; a positive feeling unites the soul with the world, while a negative feeling forces the soul back into itself, thus creating the distance from the world that alone makes judging possible. Pleasure unites, repugnance separates, and only the separation of soul from world makes it possible for the soul to know the world. Judging, therefore, is a function of the soul that enables us to know the qualities of the world as parts of the universe.

Personality as the Result of a Separation Process

The little child as a soul-being has not yet disentangled itself from the world. It really lives *with* and *in* the world; it perceives the world inwardly in the form of experiences. Soul and world are still undivided. The little child is at one with the sweet taste of the milk, with the caress of the mother, with the blue of the sky and the green of the trees. Only gradually does the process of separation come about. The birth of the soul and finally of the whole personality takes place, and in connection with this the ability to judge emerges.

37

The birth of the personality in soul and spirit is basically a process of separation. The soul must disengage itself from the universe. In every positive feeling, we give up something of our personality to merge with the universe. Judging, however, makes possible a union with the universe in which the independence of the personality is retained. Experiencing is thus the first force in the soul, embracing both positive and negative feelings. Through negative feelings, judging becomes possible. Thus we could regard the function of judging as, in a certain sense, the aspect of feeling that is directed outward, i.e., toward the world.

The Development of Judging in Connection with Language

We take the word "judgment" (*oordeel*, German *Urteil*) in a literal sense. *Oordeel* (literally, primal part) is for us a part of the All which *is* from the beginning; and the soul that judges unites itself in its knowing and recognizing with the primal parts of the world. A soul that disengages itself from the world in negative feeling can observe these primal parts and recognize them as sweet or bitter, blue or yellow, high or low, beautiful or ugly, good or bad, and so on. Along with these qualities, the growing child learns the words for the things and appearances that exhibit these qualities, words such as milk, grass, heaven, animal, man, etc. The relationships between things and their qualities are then established with words, e.g., "The grass is green; the sky is blue; the man is good," and so on.

Before learning these relationships, there lived in the child's soul a nearly undifferentiated perception of things, for example, of grass: "That which extends around me, which has a certain color, which can be touched in a certain way, and so on, is called 'grass.' " An inner recognition takes place, completed only when the right word is born in the soul.

Before the child is able to speak, he points with an inner

38

or outer gesture to the things and appearances and says "ta-ta" or "da-da." He is expressing something we could render as: "That is it! This I find here in the world! This is a part of the world of which *I* am a part, too. It belongs with me in this world." Following this, the word is born out of the soul as a happy experience. The child feels entirely satisfied only when the word that belongs specifically to an appearance arises in his soul. Only then are the relationships established. The things and appearances and their qualities are brought together through judgments: "The grass is green, grows, is juicy, has a certain smell," etc. Judging thus develops in connection with speech. The appearances of the inner and outer worlds are established by an ever-growing number of judgments in the course of speaking.

Feeling and Judging Circumscribe the Whole of the Inner Soul-Life

Feeling and judging are the two primary elements in the life of the soul. Their polar relationship is given classical expression in Goethe's remark: "While observing nature, in the large and in the small, I continually asked myself: 'Is it the object that is expressing itself, or is it you.' "[23] The soul ("you") expresses itself in feeling, the world ("the object") in judging. Steiner emphasized that the inner realm of the soul is fully determined by these two functions:

> These two conceptions—judging and differentiating love and hatred—if rightly understood, embrace the whole inner life of the soul. Everything else denotes something originating from without through the body or from within through the spiritual.[24]

We have now reached the innermost realm of the soul and we meet the first polarity between the inner kernel of man and the universe. In feeling, we experience this kernel of our being as either merged with the universe in pleasure and joy, or thrust back into itself by repugnance or suffering. In judging, the soul faces the world and proceeds from feeling to knowing and recognizing. As long as the soul lived in a feeling relationship to the world, this knowing was impossible. We cannot know something with which we are entirely united. The power of knowledge, in this case the power of judgment, comes about only by separation. The spiritual kernel of the soul makes possible a new and deeper relationship with the world as soon as the feeling relationship is extinguished.

DESIRING AND FORMING MENTAL IMAGES

Life-Forces (Drives) → *Desires* → *Feelings*

Feeling is the first process of the soul, and we have discerned that its emergence is associated with the position of the soul between "I" and "world." We must now go one step further and ask where this feeling originates. Take the example of the infant who abandons himself entirely to the qualities of the mother's milk and is fully dissolved in feelings of pleasure and satisfaction. His soul is filled with certain qualities that stream into him from the universe, stimulating the development of his bodily being and influencing it in a favorable way. His soul is connected through the senses with the qualities warm, moist, sweet, etc., all of which are recognized as good and beneficial.

The demand for life, for the development and unfolding of life, is the primal desire arising in the soul. This desire demands a feeling of pleasure and stops when pleasure is felt, as in tasting and drinking the milk. We can therefore say, at least for the moment, that desire reaches an end in feeling. In this way desiring and feeling are related as the beginning and (preliminary) end of the same process. They are different in essence but related, like a leaf with the stem and a leaf with the blossom of the same plant.

If desire is not satisfied, a feeling of irritation ensues. Ex-

40

cessive satisfaction of desire has a similar result. The child stops drinking because the feeling of pleasure becomes a feeling of dislike if he continues drinking after having satisfied the desire. The newborn baby is satisfied by the sweet taste alone. Only gradually does he encounter other tastes, such as sour, salty, and bitter. Later, depending on the extent to which the soul is fettered to the body and so to the earth, other needs arise and are satisfied by other qualities.

The intimate connection between feeling and desire has been confirmed repeatedly in the psychology of the soul ever since Thomas Aquinas. Steiner characterized the feelings as "desires thrown back into themselves, desires that have remained at a certain stage." We regard feelings here as metamorphoses of one and the same primal force, which works in the soul but shows itself in two different aspects. Between desire and feeling stands affection as a kind of transitory state in which both feeling elements and desiring elements can be found.

Desires are connected with the stream of life-forces that flow into the soul. Aristotle included them in the realm of the soul (vegetative soul). As mentioned earlier, we do not include these life-forces in the soul and will describe them later in greater detail, using the term "drives" for them. In these forces one has to seek the real driving-force: life.

The stream of life-forces expands in the soul, and where this happens desires emerge at the border between body and soul. When desires are satisfied, they give rise to positive feelings; in the opposite case, to negative feelings.

feelings ↑ desires	}	realm of the soul
life-forces ↑ (drives)	}	connected with the body

41

We have explored the origin of feelings and discovered that their inherent character points back to a preceding state, a process, from which they derive. It is different with judgments. Their origin is given directly by the relationship between soul and world. We cannot pursue this relationship further back than to the moment when the soul encounters the primal parts of the universe, which reveal themselves as qualities. The question here is not where a judgment originates, but into what does it develop? A feeling brings a desire at least to a relative end. A judgment, however, is a beginning and has the tendency to develop further. Judgments such as "The grass is green," "The tree is tall," form mental images (*vorstellingen*) in the soul: "the green grass," "the tall tree." As already mentioned, everything in the soul is in continuous movement; everything is process, activity. Just as desires are constantly absorbed into feelings, so judgments continually give rise to mental images.

The qualities of the world are manifold, with countless shades and variations. They are organized in endless ways in the phenomena of the world. Whole groups of phenomena, encountered first in our judgments, are condensed into mental images. Judgments such as "The tree is tall and green; the tree lives and grows; the tree has a trunk" (something that strives upwards, has a circumference) "and a crown of foliage" (something that expands), become mental images such as "the tall, green tree," "the living, growing tree," "the upward-striving and expanding tree," and are condensed into the mental image of "tree." The mental image, "tree," thus embodies a great number of detailed mental images, all arising out of judgments.

The soul finds a point of rest only in the general mental image, "tree," from which the word for it can be born. As long as the child is still learning to speak, he hears the sounds of the words in his surroundings and learns their use through imitation. The words are in a certain sense wider

42

than the judgments and mental images that the child gradually forms. By degrees they come to coincide completely, so that the mental image is really born *in* the word-image. In this way the judgment conforms to the mental image and thereby gains clearer outlines. As an image it is projected to the border between soul and world. The mental image is therefore an inwardly fixed judgment, showing through this inner fixity a certain finality.

We can also describe the mental image as a judgment no longer experienced in terms of the soul's acts of knowing and recognizing but "placed in front of the I" at the border between soul and world. The Dutch word *vorstelling* (German *Vorstellung*) expresses this process exactly.

Judgments find their conclusion in mental images. Previously we spoke of a *process* in the soul in which the relationship between soul and world was continuously changing. We could not live as conscious men, however, if we carried nothing but these countless judgments within us. It is therefore necessary that the judgments be fixed as mental images and carried with us in the form of nearly unchangeable images. These mental images enable us to communicate with each other through speaking. We know from words what another person means.

To summarize, we can say that in judging we have to do with a process of recognizing that takes place between soul and world, and this process leads through the forming of pictures to the establishment of enduring mental images.

Mental Images and the Mental Image of the "I"

Among these mental images there is *one* that has a special position, and this mental image is the "I." All other mental images arise in connection with phenomena that belong in one way or another to the world (including our own body and our own soul, in so far as this is linked to the world). Only the mental image of our own "I" has a different origin.

It arises independently from the innermost realm of the soul and has no causal connection with anything else.

The mental image of the "I" is unique in that it accompanies all other mental images, either quite perceptibly or more or less in the background. This means that all other mental images are in a close relationship to *one* central mental image, that of the "I."

The Place of Drives, Feelings, Judgments, and Mental Images

In desiring and forming mental images, we reach areas of the soul more or less at the border between soul and world, whereas feeling and judging take place in the middle area of the soul, as we have seen. Feelings have their origin in desires. These are at the border between the soul and bodily life. The area of the drives, i.e., the real field of life, is linked to the bodily organs. Where the life-forces stream into the soul, the drives evolve into desires. If desires are retained in the realm of the soul, they metamorphose into feelings. Judgments lead us through the formation of mental images toward the world. Forming mental images is indeed a condensation into images, but it occurs when the soul directs itself to the spirit, i.e., to the spiritual structure of the universe. It is thus a process of spiritualization, though through the condensation a severance from living spiritually occurs, so that a dead image comes into being at the border between soul and spirit.

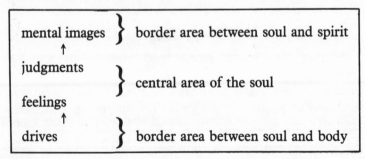

44

ACTING AND THE IMPULSE TO ACT; PERCEIVING AND SENSING

From Drives to Action; Acts Belong to the World

Until now we have described the functions that have their place in the middle of the soul or in the border-regions between soul and body or soul and spirit. We come now to two functions belonging not to the realm of the soul but directly linked to it, namely acting and perceiving. In exploring action, we will look again at the awakening life of the soul in the newly born child. Driven by its will to live, expressing itself in the soul as desire, the baby makes certain movements that soon acquire a regular and relatively controlled pattern and thus become actions. That drives and desires are a direct impulse to actions is evident if we think, for example, of sucking and grasping. Later we will discuss in more detail the various motives for actions (see Chapter III). Here it will suffice to show that the motive to act is in the soul, and indeed in the field of desires at the border between body and soul, but the action itself does not reside in the soul. With the action we leave the soul and enter the world. Once performed, an action no longer belongs to our inner being; it has entered the world and belongs to it, becoming a component part of the world.

With desires we have to do with inner movements of the soul. These movements work strongly into the body, especially into the limbs, and become outer movements. Hence they pass from the realm of the soul into that of the body. They then belong to the world, just as our body does. They enter the world in the moment when the motive for action, which lives in the soul, lays hold of the body and brings it into movement.

Desire → Feeling → Judgment → Mental Image → Perception (World); The Place of the Senses

Perception also leads us into an area that can no longer

45

be credited to the soul. In action, a movement of the soul works into the body and thus enters the world. In perception, the opposite takes place: a movement in the soul is withheld in a certain sense, creating a space for the instreaming world.

If we see something, for example, a red flower, this "something" does not belong to the soul. Neither the red color nor the form of the flower is part of our soul. The flower is in the world and belongs to the world. Perception of it becomes possible because the qualities of the world enter us through the sense-organs, the gates of the soul. The world enters through these gates and comes to the border of the soul realm.

From this point of view we can understand why the sense-organs in general show so many similarities to physical instruments. For example, the front part of the eye (cornea, iris, lens, pupil) can be compared with the corresponding part of a photographic camera. Both are built in accordance with physical laws. This comparison is no longer valid for the rear part of the eye. The retina, for example, cannot be compared with a photographic plate, for its functions are linked to the living nerve-cells and can be understood only in terms of the laws valid for them. It is the same for the ear. Here we again find the outer and middle ear conforming with the laws of physics, but a portion of the ear also relates to the life-process. In the organs of touch, one part is connected mainly with the mechanical laws, in the organs of taste, with chemical laws.

These outwardly directed parts of the sense-organs are the gates in the bodily organism through which the world is brought into direct proximity with the soul. It is, of course, not the things of the world themselves but rather their qualities that appear at the border of the soul. The meeting between soul and world takes place there. We have already described how a force working in the soul leads our judgments to the border area between soul and world, and how in this way our judgments become mental images. If perception ensues, this process is carried one stage further, outside the border-area and therefore into the world. A projection into the world takes place, rather than a culmination in a fixed mental image.

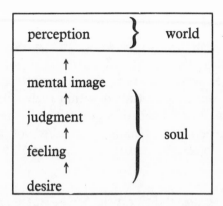

By directing itself to the outer world, the process of knowing and recognizing reaches the qualities of the world in the world itself, and thereby perception comes about. Hence perception is also a mental image projected into the world.

The Process of Perception Moves from the Internal to the External

That perception is also a mental image seemingly contradicts the generally accepted view that perceiving is a process running not from inside outwards but from outside inwards. As long as one considers only the outer factors important for perception, one can accept the ordinary view, in which you begin with phenomena of light, color, and sound, and you describe how these evoke certain reactions, more or less mechanically, physically, or chemically, in the sense-organs and in the nerves connected with them. One can never understand through this how the picture of the percept arising in the soul comes about. We can understand the process of perception only if we consider as primary the active force in the soul that is directed outwards to the world.

That we are dealing here with an active process, an outgoing function of the soul, is expressed in the Dutch word for perceiving, *waarnemen* (German *wahrnehmen*), "true taking." The soul takes something from the world into itself, and the soul "takes true," i.e., receives within itself the "truth" of phenomena in the world. In this connection one thinks of Goethe's saying: "The senses do not deceive; judgment deceives." In fact, the senses *cannot* deceive, because the world is continued within them. Only in the case of an illness or a defect does perception become untrue, as, for example, in color-blindness. So-called optical illusions and similar defects of perception are in reality errors of judgment.

The Differences among Perception, Sense-Impression, and Feeling

We must, however, make a clear distinction between perception and sense-impression (Dutch *gewaarwording*, German *Empfindung*). We can briefly articulate this difference in the following way: percepts belong to the world, sense-impressions to the soul. If we perceive something in the world, for example, a flower, this process passes over not unnoticed into the experience of our soul. When we turn our eyes away from an object we have observed, a certain impression also remains in the soul. We speak of a perception only in so far as the soul is in direct connection with the object. A sense-impression, then, is that which is left over in the soul as the result of a perception.

The soul is entirely permeated by forces that we have learned to know as feelings and desires. The feelings are active more in the middle area of the soul, the desires more in the border area between body and soul. They are mostly in

48

close proximity to the sense-organs. They wait in this border-area, so to speak, for an opportunity to unite themselves with the world. This conjunction finds expression in the process of sensing. A sense-impression is therefore caused mainly by desires working at the border between body and soul, and thus there arises the deeper, more inwardly experienced connection with the soul, which is characteristic of a sense-impression in contrast to a perception.

A perception is a mental image projected outwardly. A sense-impression arises in the same way but by withholding, by retaining the force that directs the judgment to the mental image. This restraint comes about when a desire at the border of the soul withdraws from its relationship to the world.

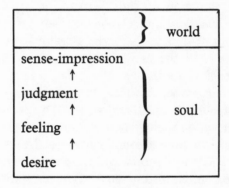

The experience of sense-impressions is thus a relatively complicated function of the soul; its component parts are judgment and desire.

Since, as we saw earlier, retained desires evolve into feelings in the soul, the affinity between sense-impressions and feelings becomes clear. We speak of sense-impressions not only in connection with sense-perceptions but also if we wish to indicate an emotion or feeling that has resulted from a relationship to the world and therefore makes a more peripheral impression on the soul (for example, a pleasant or an unpleasant impression).

The Relationships among Desires, Perceptions, and Sense-Impressions

The relationship between action and perception is shown by their relationship with the world. Both processes live outside the realm of the soul. While the motive for an action lies in the soul and the action outside it, so is a perception outside the soul and a sense-impression inside it. Desire has an important role in the formation of both. If perceptions arise more in connection with sense-processes, which have a greater importance for the bodily organism, the desire will be more strongly connected with them and the element of sense-impression more obvious. We can confirm this in ourselves if we examine the relationship between perception and sense-impression in the various realms of the senses. The more we reach the area of vital processes, the greater is the role of sense-impressions.

We can, for example, successively imagine perceptions of a color, a sound, a smell, and a taste. The perception of a color as such is, on the whole, hardly connected at all with desire. The sense-impression it makes on the soul remains generally weak. Most people will have great trouble in expressing the content of this sense-impression, even though the perception of the color could not be more distinct. The perception of tones and sounds evokes more the element of desire. The soul is moved in its deeper layers and the emotional life is stirred. In perceptions of smell and taste, the soul is directly involved in the border area where desires are active, so that the sense-impression element is dominant. It will be possible later, when we describe the realm of the senses, to clarify this from another perspective.

50

III. A More Detailed Description of the Forces at Work in the Soul

The Relationship between the Different Soul Forces

The description of the forces at work in the soul, given in the preceding chapter, is of course schematic. Events in the soul form a great, interrelated whole. All the forces of the soul are continuously tied to one another, while at the same time they all revolve around the kernel of the spiritual and moral personality, which we described previously as the "I." The sum of these forces working together is in the service of the "I," which makes use of them during the life between birth and death.

Many students of the soul have believed it possible to deduce the complicated functions of soul-life from so-called "simple elements." This was an atomistic prejudice related to the erroneous assumption that a natural scientific approach, and indeed a very closely defined one, could be applied to the life of the soul. In reality, there are no "pure sense-impressions," no "simple feelings," and the like. In every mental image, elements of judgment, feeling, and desire are present. Similarly, in every feeling and desire the other elements of the soul are also present. This has been proved in modern psychology by investigations showing that in each function of the soul-life, in each process, there is more living activity than can be understood by considering only the single components. This is because everything in the soul is related to the kernel of the personality, the "I," and is ruled primarily by the "I." We should therefore look on every function, every process that works in the soul, as a modification of the primal, divine-spiritual forces that always accompany the kernel of the personality. Later it will be possible to describe the nature of these divine-

51

spiritual forces. Their existence has already been noted in Chapter I. It is now necessary to describe their activity in the depth of the life of the soul. We find spiritual forces in all human life, where they take hold of body, soul, and spirit in such a way that they work in a circumscribed manner in the body and the life-processes, while in the soul they awaken and unfold so as to reveal their essential nature in the life of the spirit.

FEELING

The World Lives in the Soul or the Soul is Closed to the World; Feeling

In the previous chapter we explored feeling as the force directly related to the soul's ability to open or close itself in relation to its surroundings in an inner movement of the soul, a kind of inner gesture. This movement, this gesture, is primary in the life of the soul. We can also call it a yes-no movement or gesture. If the soul opens in the yes-movement, it is permeated by the world-content to which it opens itself. This permeation leads to an experience of an inner merging quality with the universe, which can be experienced as life-enhancing, beneficial, and therefore agreeable and joyful. With a no-movement, the opposite takes place. The soul closes itself, defends itself inwardly, and thereby comes to experience itself. It divides itself from the world and thus places itself in opposition to the world. As we said previously, this makes judging possible.

It is interesting to draw attention to the main sounds of the words "yes" (Dutch and German *ja*) and "no" (Dutch *neen*, German *nein*). From the point of view of spiritual science, the ah-sound is the expression characteristic for the opening soul. One could say that the ah-sound comes about if the soul does nothing but open itself inwardly, thereby bringing this process itself to expression. Call to mind, for example, the times when a man says "ah," without knowing why, in astonishment, bewilderment, surprise, and the like. For the little child just beginning to express itself, the "ah" is also characteristic.

The eh-sound, however, is formed when the outwardly directed stream of speech is compressed in its rising. Through this retention, the eh-sound forms by itself. Man also says "ae," ("ah," "eh") if something hits him rudely and he wants to throw this something "out" of himself. The crying of a baby is distinctly tuned to the ae-sound, whereas human laughter is based on the ah-sound, at least if it comes from the heart.

When the soul opens itself to the world and is permeated by its qualities, positive feelings result. In the opposite case, we experience negative feelings. Hence we could characterize positive feelings as what the soul experiences when it accepts the contents of the world and unites with them and the negative feelings as experiences in which the contents of the world are rejected. Union with the world, becoming one with the world, is experienced in one case; being divided from the world, facing the world, in the other case. In other words: the world lives within the soul, or the soul experiences itself outside the world. To be able to experience this opposition inwardly is the real characteristic of feeling.

Pleasure–Displeasure; Sympathy–Antipathy;
Joy–Sorrow; Love–Hate

If we now try to order the various ways in which feelings show themselves in the soul, we find pleasure–displeasure feelings dependent on the body, and also, in a certain sense, at the border between feeling and desiring. Here we are dealing with feelings connected in one way or another with bodily experiences, for example, needs and wants of the body, such as hunger and thirst, the need for warmth and coolness, for fresh air, and the like; sexual desires also belong here. They all give rise to feelings of pleasure if they are satisfied or to feelings of displeasure if they are not.

In the feelings indicated by the words sympathy and antipathy, we enter more into the realm of the soul itself. In these words the elements of uniting and withdrawing are directly expressed. One distinguishing aspect of these feelings, as opposed to feelings of pleasure and displeasure, is that they have more lasting significance for the soul. Feelings of pleasure and displeasure may be strong or even vehement, but they are soon forgotten. When hunger is appeased, the feeling of pleasure vanishes almost at once, leaving only a certain satisfaction or ease. Its value for the life of the soul is small. In the experience of sympathy and antipathy, however, the soul as a whole is moved to greater activity. A strong sympathy or antipathy occupies or fills the soul-life for a longer period.

Feelings of joy and sorrow are in the same category; they, too, belong to the soul itself. They are distinguished from feelings of sympathy and antipathy in that they indicate a state of the soul as such and emerge less clearly from a particular origin. In joy and sorrow something of a more objective nature is expressed.

Feelings of love and hatred are still more complex and also deeper, in the sense that not only the whole soul but also the spiritual–moral personality is engaged. These feelings appear in many different forms and shades, e.g., in love for nature, for the fatherland or native place, for a child or other members of the family, for a beloved one or good friend. In each case the feeling is composed in a particular way. In love for nature, a certain bodily feeling of pleasure can play a role, but a true love for nature is something far superior. Similarly, love for one's native country can be an elementary bodily attachment or a high moral feeling. This is also true of family relationships. Love for a child can have a strong tinge of animal instinct, but it can also express the blessedness and wonder of watching the growing personality.

In the love-relationship between man and woman, this whole scale of feelings can be discerned: emerging bodily drives and demands that give rise to positive feelings of pleasure in the realm of the senses; but also a deeper relationship that can fill the entire soul; feelings of love that can lead to the highest imaginable ecstasy; and the love that grows in the inner tranquillity of the soul into an ever-stronger force, giving the soul the strength for complete dedication and sacrifice, the highest and deepest inner values.

The stronger the attachment of love to the body, the greater the role of desire. In this case we have the "love that blinds." The more that love becomes liberated in the realm of the soul, the more it takes root in the moral, spiritual personality, thus becoming a bestowing love. One thus reaches the love that "opens the eyes."[25]

In relation to a good friend or to our fellow men in general, the feeling of love arises from less tension. Forces of desire linked to the body are not involved so strongly. Hence the feeling is generally less intense, and strong moral and spiritual motives must work in the soul if such a love is to flourish. This is even more the case in the realm of the impersonal or supra-personal where we are concerned with love for an ideal, or for truth and virtue.[26]

We can regard pure Christian love as the highest form of love, in which a sacrifice of the whole personality is made in freedom for the salvation of mankind.

The Ordering of Feelings

The question of whether feelings have more than one dimension, which for a long time played a part in the study of psychology, has contributed little to a better understanding of the soul. The whole idea of dimension is misleading here, for it leaves no room for the concept of the development of feelings in the polar relationship of body and spirit. The significance of the pleasure–displeasure opposition is that it allows us to see effects limited to a certain area of the soul. We cannot immediately deduce all other feelings from this opposition, but this is possible if we add two other pairs to the pleasure–displeasure feelings, as Wundt did in his theory of three-dimensionality: pleasure–displeasure, excitation–appeasement; tension–relaxation.

Scheler employed a much more effective method in his attempt to order the feelings according to the areas in which they unfold their activity.[27] He distinguished between "sensuous feeling," "vital feeling," the feelings belonging to the realm of the spiritual, and finally those relevant to the highest inner qualities, which he associated with the opposition "holy–unholy." Scheler's first category includes everything related to the opposites pleasant–unpleasant, in so far as the experience is linked with our sensual nature. The second category includes all feelings related to the sphere of "well-being or welfare." The third category includes the phenomena of "love and hatred," which are related to the sphere of the beautiful and the ugly, right or wrong, the true and the untrue. The fourth group, finally, is related only to the sphere of "absolute things," i.e., forces, persons, or institutions that rank as holy. Feelings of blessedness or despair can arise in this connection. In Scheler's ordering of the feelings, one can clearly see an attempt to study the developing feelings and to make visible something of the spiritual–moral stages with which the developing soul is engaged.

The Human Being and "Pure Feeling"

All the forms of feelings characterized up to now can be seen as gradual revelations of one of the three spiritual primal forces attending the "I." (One might also call it one of the three ways in which the "I" reveals itself.) We call this primal force "pure feeling," meaning the feeling that can hover before man as his highest ideal, in other words: "real feeling," a divine–spiritual archetypal force, of which

56

man experiences the various adumbrations while he is bound to his earthly personality. If pure feeling were to develop fully in the human soul, the soul would become an organ capable of revealing in the human being the highest possible forces in the spiritual domain.

As light appears to the human soul by means of the eye, so would the forces of sympathy and antipathy, in their highest form of joy and sorrow, mold the soul into an organ to perceive divine love and also to perceive everything opposed to this love. Man lives in this pure feeling as if in an immense cosmic-earthly rhythm. The highest conceivable tension between "universe" and "I" comes to expression therein. Out of the original union or relationship between "I" and "universe," the personality breaks free at birth and proceeds, through a continually advancing process of individualization, to detach itself increasingly from the universe. In the movements of feelings, union with the universe is attained and dissolved repeatedly, but the union is at first imperfect. A positive feeling can fill the soul entirely for a time, as, for example, enthusiasm for a good deed, or complete self-surrender in a love-relationship. These feelings are transient, however. A really enduring relationship with the universe develops only if the whole personality unites itself with the universe through sacrifice by means of Christian love. Nevertheless, something of this immense mystery is experienced in every positive feeling, however small.

Desire and Satisfaction; Judgment and Decision;
Impatience, Hope, Doubt

The character of feelings is determined mainly by the course of soul-processes. Whether or not a certain desire is satisfied is decisive for the kind of feeling connected with it. As desire comes to an end in satisfaction, judgment comes to an end in decision. In our soul, a number of more or less latent judgments on the same fact or question are always present. At a certain moment, when the judgment is completed in one or more mental images, a decision is made.

Decision as such is an element alien to the soul, as Steiner mentioned.[28] The significance of a mental image is that it gives expression to a truth. The soul itself, however, does not determine truth, as we mentioned earlier. The truth of things and phenomena is given as a spiritual fact. So long as we are inwardly concerned with the rightness of our judgment, we are still living in the realm of the soul. A decision brings us into relationship with truth, unites us, indeed, with the truth, therefore leading us out of the realm of the soul.

In the satisfaction of desires we do indeed live in the soul, but desires have their origin outside the soul. In this connection, Steiner distinguished between man as "enjoyer" and man as "fighter."[29] He is a fighter with regard to judgment, an enjoyer with regard to desire. A large part of our feeling-life is connected with the search for satisfaction and decision. The feeling of impatience, for example, arises from desiring a satisfaction that does not come. In hope, we have a stream of desire-forces evenly permeated by an element of judgment. Desire and judgment are in a certain balance. The desire is awaiting satisfaction, the judgment is awaiting a decision. With doubt, the case is again different. Here the force of judgment is too weak to give rise to a decision. The soul is therefore suspended in an indeterminate state of feeling originating in a desire, a longing for certainty.

DESIRING

Drives in Plant, Animal, and Man; Desire,
Wish, Longing, Will; "Pure Willing"

We have already discussed on pp. 40–41 the relationship between feeling and desiring, and we attributed the emergence of feelings to the effect of desires in the soul. Besides this, we were able to order the feelings according to the area of the soul to which they are related—to the border-area between body and soul, to the realm of the soul itself, or to the border-area between soul and spirit.

In a similar way we can now order the desires that work in the soul, for here also we are dealing with a whole array of manifestations. First of all we will take the drives at work in the human organism as forces of nature. Just as a life-impulse, a drive to grow and develop, to be nourished and to propagate, permeates the entire vegetative world, so does a sum of life-impulses work in the entire human organism, whereby the vegetative nature in man can develop. All this is perceptible in the soul. These drives unfold in the unconscious life of the organs.

In man these driving-forces are also forces of growth, metabolism, and the like. Only where the element of desire unites with the drive does the soul actively participate in it. In nature this happens with the animals, but one can only assume that it does with the higher animals. The process of growth and development in the plant-world is without desire. The plant's growth forces are entirely merged in the becoming and forming of the plant itself. The plant reveals in its entire form the complexity of the growth-forces. For these reasons Goethe was able to read the laws of life, of the development of life and its unfolding, in the plant.

Animals, however, are quite different. The animal form does not immediately reveal the whole complex of growth-forces; instead it exemplifies the animal's dominating desires. The appearance of the wolf is thus a bodily expression of the particular desires that animate this animal. Similarly, the horse, the cow, the birds, all illustrate their characteristic desires in their bodily formations. In the plant, accordingly, we can speak only of life-forces, while in the animal the element of soul appears in the form of desires.

The life-impulse mentioned above was described by

59

Scheler as the "lowest stage of the psychic," which appears outwardly as "living being" and inwardly as "soul." He regarded this as the force that makes everything move, supplying the "power behind every activity, even behind the most luminous heights of spiritual activity." For this force he used the name "feeling-drive" (*Gefühlsdrang*), combining feeling and drive in a single word.[30]

On page 26 we pointed out that it seems better to make a sharper distinction between body and soul unless one prefers, as Aristotle did, to arrange the soul in a number of planes or spheres, the lowest of which embraces the realm of life. In our considerations we shall speak of soul-functions only where "life" becomes "experience," i.e., when life-impulses become emotional movements by flowing into desires.

We have seen how these desires work in the animal. In man, they work in the border-area between body and soul, in close connection with the drives. They strive in the first place to obtain food and similar things making for bodily comfort. Such desires also work strongly in sexual relations. Indeed, they are active wherever a man desires something that will directly satisfy his body and soul. He can, for example, desire wealth and prosperity, a good position, celebrity, honor, and so on.

If a certain liberation of the forces of desire takes place in the soul, we no longer speak of desire but rather of wish and longing. Wish and longing are not tied to the body in the way that drives are, and there is a difference also in their intensity. A wish has on the whole a subtler quality and is more transient. Longing fills the soul to a greater extent. In the word "longing" we experience something of that inner "lengthening" of the soul as it reaches towards that for which it longs.

If the desire not only has been released in the soul but rises further into the realm of the spirit, it reveals itself there as *will*. By contrast with what we often call "will" in ordinary life, we will speak here of "pure willing." In this pure willing we meet the archetypal spiritual force that accompanies the "I," as with pure feeling. This pure willing is closely associated with the spiritual–moral kernel of our personality. It thus works in our soul primarily in three different ways: through its link to the body in the desires; through unfolding in the soul as wish and longing; and showing its real nature in pure willing. In speaking of pure feeling, we drew attention to the immense archetypal rhythm that is thereby revealed and that expresses the relationship between world and "I." Pure willing is the first principle, the beginning of all, the spiritual-dynamic starting-point of all human evolution in terms of body, soul, and spirit.

From this point of view, therefore, pure willing is an older force than pure feeling. In a certain sense, as we have seen, feeling is born out of willing. If, however, we consider the relationship of feeling and willing to the soul-life itself, as we will later in speaking about consciousness, we must describe the will as a less conscious, even an unconscious, force. We know less about our own will than we do about our life of feeling. Ordinary human consciousness does not yet extend deeply enough to penetrate the realm where the will is active.

The Relationship between Willing and Feeling

Because it is the nature of the will to be hidden, the will has been entirely ignored as an independent force in the soul during a recent period in the history of psychology.[31] In fact, feeling was also accepted only as an accompaniment of mental images and other soul contents. Feeling was not regarded as an independent force but apparently had independence only as a so-called "feeling tone." Recognition of the will, on the other hand, disappeared entirely during this period. What had been discovered in the soul as a so-called will-force was wholly attributed to reflex-movements in the body, which then, of course, acquired a very complicated character. Psychology before this period, and now modern

61

psychology, have recognized the independent nature of feeling as well as of the will.

Brentano took a remarkable position, defending a union of the two categories, feeling and willing.[32] This had already been done in the Scholastic period by Thomas Aquinas, among others.[33] Brentano thought that the union of these two forces reveals itself through inner experience. He pointed to intermediate states between the feelings of pleasure and displeasure on the one hand and willing on the other. As an example he gave the following sequence: "Sadness—longing for the missing good—hope that it may be attained—desire to get it—courage to search for it—decision of the will to take action."[34] On the one side is a feeling, sadness; on the other a decision of the will. They are seemingly very distant from each other but are closely linked by the intermediary aspects. The transition is therefore nearly imperceptible.

A fundamental error is made, however, in concluding that these nearly imperceptible transitions indicate a similarity of the categories to which the two extremes belong. Between yellow and blue one could find a number of shades that make a gradual transition, and many other examples could be given of the subtle gradation between extremes. The countless shades of intermediary aspects are possible when the two extremes belong to one realm. Yellow and blue are both colors; desiring and feeling are both forces of the soul. As the soul is a great, united whole, transitions between the various categories of the life of the soul can always be shown.

Brentano's second argument is also unsatisfactory. He spoke about the way in which the two forces, feeling and desiring, relate to objects. For him, feeling and desiring are connected in a similar way with their objects, and in his opinion the essential factor is the phenomenon of love and hatred in its manifold revelations. In fact, however, this ignores that in essence feeling and desiring can be assigned to different categories, for the relationships they have respectively to their objects are, in a certain sense, polar opposites. Desire and pleasure-through-satisfaction (or, in the case of a negative feeling, displeasure through non-satisfaction) are related to each other as a question is to an answer. If a child desires milk and experiences a feeling of comfort when this desire is satisfied, but feels uncomfortable in the opposite case, then such feelings are the consequence of the desire and are linked with it only in this way. This intimate relationship between the two categories leads to Brentano's error that there is no real difference between them. The relationship between feeling and desiring resembles that between mother and child. The mother is necessary for the earthly birth of the child, but the child is an individuality on its own account. Steiner characterized this genetic connection by speaking about feeling as a "will withheld within itself." This is not meant to imply that the categorical difference between the two should be ignored but is to be understood in such a way that feeling is a younger element that can come to function independently in the whole personality only if the will, from which it originates, is withheld.

ACTING

Movement (Involuntary and Reflexive) and Actions

In exploring action, we enter an area lying essentially outside the soul, as mentioned earlier. The preparation for action, however, lies in the soul itself. The best way to understand action is as a movement in the soul that continues as a bodily process (mainly as a movement of the limbs) and merges with the body. An inner soul-movement thus reaches from *out* of the soul *into* the body, i.e., into the world, and becomes a part of the world. Our emotions, feelings, desires, and the like belong to our inner world, our actions to the outer world. Emotional movements, like all functions of the soul, are associated with bodily processes, as we will

63

describe later. The difference between emotional movements and action is that in emotional movements the soul expands beyond the bodily processes but does not merge with the body. The relationship between soul-movement and bodily process continues in emotion, whereas in action the bodily process takes over the soul-movement entirely.

The most elementary bodily movements are all involuntary movements of the muscles associated with vital processes, for example, movements of the heart, blood corpuscles, respiratory organs, stomach, intestines, etc. They originate in the life-processes as such and thus in the life-instincts. In normal healthy life these movements remain entirely unconscious. They are perceptible only when disturbances occur, and then they are felt as discomfort, pain, cramps, and the like. The harmonious working of life-instincts and movement is therefore generally imperceptible in the life of the soul. Only if a disturbance occurs are they divided, and the soul then realizes its inability to merge with the life-process.

Closely related to these involuntary movements are reflex movements. The baby makes these movements when it is drinking, but it will also grasp a finger touching its hands, and it will turn its head to the light. The movements of the adult who blinks in the light, withdraws his hand from the hot stove, and so on, are also reflexes. We can regard them as movements related on the one hand to the life-instincts and on the other to the desires at work in the soul. In laughing man expands his soul and relaxes his features. The contrast between "uniting/withdrawing" or "self-giving/self-defense" is expressed in them. Also important in this regard are laughing and weeping, mentioned previously. Through this relaxation the features become less sharp, the skin reddens, and so the expression of the face becomes at the same time both softer and more lively. In weeping, on the other hand, the soul withdraws either gradually or with

64

cramp-like shocks. This contracting soul-movement passes over to the lachrymal glands. Weeping brings about a certain relaxation, since in this way a movement emerges from the soul. The soul is, so to speak, relieved.

The movements become actions if they arise from within the realm of the soul, that is, if desires, wishes, and longing are their originating cause and lead the will to perform a certain action. Actions can also be caused by other forces in the soul, such as feelings of pleasure and displeasure, sympathy and antipathy, joy and sorrow, love and hatred. Certain images and thoughts must also be mentioned here. Under the influence of high ideals and moral emotions, an action can ascend to the height of a sacrifice; in that case, not only the inner movement of the soul passes over to the limbs but the soul itself goes out *with* the movements and offers itself to the world.

Play; "The Drives of Matter, of Form, and of Play: Freedom" (Schiller)

We must give special attention to the movements and actions that appear in play. A healthy child feels a need to play at an early age. As the child grows older, play will become more complicated and can develop, according to the nature of the child, in various directions. One characteristic, however, is always predominant: play always deals with life in a polarity of creating and dissolving forms.

Nobody, perhaps, has explored the essence of play more deeply than Schiller in his *Letters on the Aesthetic Education of Man*, in which he described the "drive to play" (*Spieltrieb*) as the essential force through which man can reveal himself as a freely creative being.[35] Schiller began with two powerful influences or "drives" that dominate human existence: the influence of material necessity (*Sachtrieb* or *Stofftrieb*), originating in physical nature, including the sense-nature of man; and the influence of rational or form-giving necessity (*Formtrieb*), bound up with man's spiritual and intellectual nature.

The influence of material necessity tends to hold man in the constraints of time and to make him a material being. "With unbreakable bonds it fetters the upward-striving mind to the world of the senses."[36] The influence of the form-giving mind, of rational necessity, tends to liberate man from these constraints and to relate him to the eternal values of goodness and truth.

Man is bound by both these "drives," in one case to a natural world-order and in the other to a spiritual world-order. A third force that could mediate between the two is unthinkable, but where these two drives encounter each other is the place where human existence begins to be truly human. "Since two fundamentally opposed forces are active within man, they both lose their compulsion, and the opposition of two necessities gives rise to *freedom*." This freedom is manifest in what Schiller calls the "drive to play." This is a fundamental insight, not only for learning more about play in the narrower sense but for an understanding of art and of the still more difficult "art of living." "For, to put it plainly, man plays only when he is man in the fullest sense of the word, and *he is entirely man only when he 'plays.'* "[37]

V.D. Leeuw came to a similar conclusion when he said: "Man is never finished; he is continually becoming; he becomes man only in play. He is always in movement; he always goes back and forth between world (God) and himself . . . Only in playing, i.e., creating space and time, building a world, facing opposition, does man become man."[38]

The play of the child shows continual search for a mobile balance between the "drive of matter" and the "drive of form," between transcience and eternity, between form-dissolving and form-giving. The creative force of the personality becomes visible here, obviously, in a different manner but endowed with immense energy. A healthy child plays constantly and indefatigably. Through play he manipulates things in the world—he plays with his feet, with a strand of wool, with his food, with a piece of wood, later with his toys—and in so doing brings into play the highest force, the creative force with which the whole soul will soon be able to express itself through thinking, feeling, and willing in all realms of life.

JUDGING

Original Judgment; Spiritual, Aesthetic, and
Moral Judgment; Forming Judgments

Unlike feeling, which we described as a function of the soul and therefore concerned with experience, we discovered that judging is a discerning and recognizing activity. As we mentioned on p. 37, it is in judging that we distinguish between "I" and the "world." This distinction leads in the first place to establishing the existence of things or phenomena and their qualities, for outside the soul we find many important things belonging to the world in which we exist. After this comes the need to determine the positions in space and time of that which we find outside ourselves. The primary judgment is whether an appearance *exists, is,* as when a child, pointing to a stone or tree, says "stone," "tree." This implies "There lies a stone," or "There stands a tree," and is therefore a judgment referring to space. Something similar happens in relation to time, particularly in the experience of "before" or "after," "now" and "soon," and the like.

In the third place, certain relationships are established. The phenomenon "stone" and the quality "hard" meet in the judgment, "The stone is hard." The same is true with judgments such as "The sky is blue," "The child is small," etc. It is tempting to begin speaking here of "true" judgments, for at this stage, where certain relationships are expressed, the possibility of false judgments arises. If one considers here the possibility of false judgments, then one assumes judging to be a cognizing, distinguishing function; judgments in which such a relationship is expressed are, however, nothing but a composite of the original judgments.

In ordinary speech, and also in psychology, we speak of "judging" if we wish to establish a truth in the area of reason and understanding or in the aesthetic and moral realms, i.e., where true or untrue, beautiful or ugly, good or bad, come into question. In these judgments we have to do with composite soul-functions that engage the full attention of the soul. The soul must also undergo a development in this area, as we will now show. Composite judgments reach a definite conclusion only if a decision is reached after inner reflection, i.e., an inner process in which the whole soul takes part. Through this decision the soul unites itself with the fact or incident in question. If it is a judgment of understanding or reason in the deeper sense, the fact or incident is experienced by the soul in such a way that nothing intervenes any longer between the "I" and the "world." This can be made clear by a simple mathematical example. That $2 \times 2 = 4$ is a fact is directly experienced by the soul. The arithmetical ability existing in the soul enables it to recognize the truth of this fact. In the case of more complex arithmetical or mathematical truths, development of this power of judgment is required, but no essentially different element is involved.

In questions that arise outside the exact formulations of arithmetic, mathematics, and the like, however, the soul has to fight certain desires, feelings, etc. that make it more difficult to reach true judgments. Previous judgments and mental images, which for one reason or another are dear to the soul, can have the same hindering effect. The point is that the forces active in the soul, such as desires, feelings, as well as judgments charged with desires and feelings, must submit themselves to external truth, namely the *truth of the existing world*, which is as it is. In forming a true judgment, something that is part of the experiencing and desiring soul is sacrificed for the sake of the cognitive functions. For a judgment based on reason, this may require a long process of development. Certain judgments on the relationships in nature and the universe can be acquired only after long and intensive spiritual schooling.

In forming aesthetic judgments, something different occurs. Here desire and experience are a necessary part of judgment, but it is essential that desire be directed not to gaining possession of the object but to achieving satisfaction in perceiving it. Hence the desire remains in the sphere of the senses and unites there with judgment. Desire and judgment reach a balance that gives rise to harmony in the soul and evokes a feeling of pure joy. Aesthetic judgments of this kind come about through the enjoyment of the beauty of nature or art. The desire in the soul finds satisfaction here not through a feeling of pleasure linked to the body but rather, because the desire is satiated, at the border of the soul in the sense-perception through judgment.[39]

Moral or ethical judgment is a process similar to that already described in speaking of judgment through understanding or reason. The difference is that in moral judgment the desiring soul does not give itself over to the truth of the world *around us* but to the truth of *the spirit within us*. Just as in the first case a state should be attained where nothing intervenes any more between "I" and "world," so in the latter case a state must be attained in which the "I" and the "inner world" of the spirit face each other directly. The point here is that the "I" must feel itself directly united with the forces of "pure willing" in such a way that all feelings and desires that might intervene are suspended by this union or withdrawn.

In forming judgments through understanding and reason, the desiring and experiencing soul gives itself over to the truth of the world, whereby the "I" can reach the realm of "pure thinking." In forming aesthetic judgments, a state of inner balance between desire and judgment is attained, whereby "pure feeling" finds a place in the soul and the "I" can connect itself with it. In moral judgments, finally, the "I" is directly in the realm of "pure willing."

FORMING MENTAL IMAGES

Mental Images

On pp. 42–43 we described the forming of mental images in connection with the activity of judging and pointed out that both have a cognizing function in the soul, the opposite of desiring and feeling. The difference between judging and forming mental images, however, is that judging borders very closely on experiencing, since it arises almost simultaneously with feeling. Both originate in the innermost part of the soul. Judging represents in a certain sense the outwardly directed aspect of feeling. In forming mental images, as with desiring, we reach a more peripheral part of the soul, whereby our relationship to the surrounding world is clearly established. Here the soul lives nearer to the objects in question.

The relationship between judging and forming mental images must be understood in such a way that the latter is seen more as a final state, a state of fixity. A judgment, existing in a state of relative formlessness in the center of the soul, becomes a mental image when it moves inwardly towards the surrounding world and focuses attention on the object. As we said earlier, judgments such as, "The grass is green," "The child is small," "The tower is high," and so on, pass into the mental images, "The green grass," "The small child," "The high tower." The stream of cognizing forces thus finds a resting-place in the mental image. An inner process comes to rest, i.e., something dynamic passes into a static state. An *event* becomes a *picture*.

A certain maturity of soul is evident if a man speaks more out of his mental images than out of his judgments, but at the same time this implies a lower degree of mobility, of inner participation.[40] In judgments reached after reflection, therefore, maturity will be associated with the existence of a large number of mental images. A child's judgments, on the other hand, refer directly to his inner experience.

The mental image of the "I," described on pp. 43-44, emerges in the same way as other mental images, in so far as the relationship to judging is concerned. The only difference is that all other mental images are related in one way or another to the outer world, to the extent to which this is perceived by the senses, or to the inner world, which reveals itself in the depths of the soul. The mental image of the "I" is not directly related to either of these but springs, so to speak, from the middle of the soul. It is an experience of the "existence" of this "I" that has come to rest independently of the outer and inner worlds. Hence we must distinguish the mental image of the "I" from all other experiences one has of this "I"—for example, when one experiences, feels, or confirms that the "I" is present in the soul. The mental image of the "I" has the characteristic, already noted, of accompanying other mental images, and indeed all the other soul-functions, even if these are sometimes latent.

Forming mental images is generally a very complicated activity, an interweaving of forces involving much of the soul-life. A mental image is the outcome of a soul-process that has finally come to rest and is fixed in the form of a picture. Only young children and very primitive men have relatively simple mental images. In the more mature man, a great deal of inner experience, even a considerable part of his life, is refined in the process of forming mental images. Think of mental images such as fatherland, family, or church; still richer and more highly elaborated are the mental images used by philosophers, artists, and scholars.

Because mental images have come to rest as fixed end-states in the soul, an objective ground is established for spiritual relationships among human beings. In oral and

71

written communication, we use mental images as more or less fixed points of support. The forces of feeling and will, by blending with our mental images, can bring warmth and depth into this communication; without the fixed spiritual content of the mental images, however, all precision would be lacking.

If they emphasize the fixity of mental images, this does not mean that they cannot be developed further and, in fact, the opposite is true. Fixity is only relative. Mental images are fixed with regard to the other soul-functions, but they are continuously open to change. It is a bad sign if a man remains bound once and for all to mental images he has formed. The more he strives for inner and outer development, the more his mental images will change. Old mental images, losing their usefulness, are forgotten or remain as dim memories in the soul.

Mental Images, Feeling, and Desire;
The Hunger for Knowledge; Boredom

In the whole complex of human soul-functions, we are concerned with inner movement, change, and development. Mental images, though relatively fixed, are also subject to these processes; they too have their own life. This life of mental images depends on the fact, already mentioned, that all forces in the soul are closely linked with one another in myriad ways. In every mental image, for instance, there is an element of feeling, perceptible in the fact that the mental image is either more or less dear to us.

An element of desire also plays a part. The nature of this latter relationship is very peculiar, as Steiner pointed out.[41] Mental images evoke in the human soul a feeling of being either satiated or unsatiated. Having developed a certain activity in spiritual or intellectual areas, the soul feels satiated with mental images. There may even be a feeling of over-saturation if this activity has been forced upon the soul. In the opposite case, if one does too little spiritual or intellectual work, a feeling of not being satiated ensues. This is then experienced as a kind of hunger or thirst, engendering the common phrase, hunger or thirst for knowledge.

If the feeling of not being satiated does not rise fully into consciousness but remains dormant in the subconscious part of the soul, the peculiar phenomenon of boredom appears. The mental images then make a demand in the soul for completion and enrichment by means of desire linked to the mental images. The simple peasant, accustomed to living with but a few mental images to which he is entirely united, is less exposed to boredom than is the educated man or the town dweller, who has, indeed, a larger number of mental images, but in whom the images generally have a more superficial form. Through spiritual and intellectual activity, boredom can be overcome.

There is a remarkable similarity between the soul's need for mental images and the body's need for nourishment. In both cases, the same feeling of hunger occurs. Just as the body gains new forces from eating and drinking, so the soul strengthens itself when it engages in activities by which new mental images are formed or existing ones filled out. Novalis was no doubt pointing to this connection when he wrote, "Boredom is hunger."[42]

Judging and "Pure Thinking"

We have described the various circumstances in which appear desire, born out of the force of "pure willing," and feelings in all their forms, born from "pure feeling." In the same way, the two faculties of judging and forming mental images arise from "pure thinking." Pure thinking shows itself already in the most elementary functions of cognition and begins to unfold in simple judging. It comes to full flower only with the emergence of spiritual and moral judgments. Here we encounter the third spiritual force that accompanies the "I." Pure thinking and pure willing stand in

73

a certain sense as polar opposites to one another. While pure willing is the spiritual-dynamic principle from which the soul draws the driving-force for its development, pure thinking is the force enabling the soul to arrive at a real spiritual picture of the world, in order finally to learn the truth of the world.

No new category in the life of the soul emerges when mental images are formed from judgments, for mental images can be seen as processes of crystallization in the stream of judging and thinking. Just as salt in solution belongs to no other chemical category than that of crystallized salt, so mental images as fixed judgments belong to no other category of the soul.

For this reason, we cannot employ Brentano's three categories, feeling, judging, and forming mental images. In feeling and desiring, we have two different categories related to each other in the same way as desire and satisfaction, question and answer. This element of interplay, however, is entirely lacking in the relationship between judging and forming mental images. They are essentially of the same nature, of the same inner spiritual substance, differing only in their manifestations.

Desire as the Child in the Soul's Life; Forming Mental Images as the Old Man; Cosmically It Is the Reverse

Just as we described feeling and desiring as older and younger stages of development, so we can now determine the place of judging and forming mental images from this same point of view. We must distinguish, however, between a soul-function that has worked as a force throughout human development and the appearance of this force in the consciousness of individuals.

It is understandable that we described desiring as the eldest force in the soul, considering that in both the child and primitive man it is the first force to appear, and that it

74

then, as it were, rules the soul-life. In a little child the element of desire lives entirely in the sphere of perception, permeating it. Primitive man is also filled with this element, so that his habits of life are determined by it. Regarding human consciousness, on the other hand, desire is a young force on which thought and inner maturity have had almost no formative influence. Mental images, by contrast, can rightly be called old, since they are the most formed and fixed elements in the soul. In the complex evolution of humanity, however, mental images are nonetheless young, as they appeared only late in the process of development. In our own soul-life we can describe desire as the child within us, forming mental images as the man of advanced age, and feeling and judgment as middle-aged. Seen from the side of cosmic development, it is the other way around; there, desire is the old man and forming mental images the child. Feeling and judgment are again in the middle.

PERCEIVING

Action and Perception

In pp. 45 to 47, we came to view perception and action as functions arising in connection with the soul but taking their course in the world outside it. We saw how action comes about in connection with desiring and its manifold modifications, for the movement of the soul continues into the limbs and thus becomes part of the external world. In perceiving, the opposite takes place: the soul withdraws so that the world can stream in through the senses, which are built like gates on the frontier of the soul. Whereas in acting, an inner soul-movement flows into the world, in perceiving, something from the world streams into the soul, uniting itself with the life of the soul.

We pointed to the relationship of perceiving with the forming of mental images when we described perception as a mental image projected into the external world. The mental image, as a condensed and fixed judgment, remains within the borders of the soul-life. It is kept in the soul as a picture of what the soul experienced in judging something in the world. If this experience is brought into the world, however, then it forms itself into perception.

It is obvious, as we have said repeatedly, that here we have to do with a highly composite function, in which other forces of the soul also participate. In a brief formulation such as this, attention is drawn mainly to the dynamic principle involved. The part played by desire in perception is therefore of the greatest importance. The most significant part of human desiring lies on the borders of the sense-world. In the field of perception, accordingly, the soul lives in immediate contact with the world. Soul and world stand facing each other directly.

The Soul Perceives; The Sphere of the Senses; Disturbing Influences from Other Soul-Forces

To regard perception as an outward projection of mental images is to emphasize the inward activity of the soul expressed in outward movement. In standard psychology today, the process of perceiving is described in quite a different way, and it is indeed possible to give an account of perception by starting from outside the soul. In that case one describes how the phenomena of light, tone, odor, etc., give rise in the sense-organs to formations that are condensed in the soul into mental images. The apparent contradiction between these two ways of viewing perception disappears if we consider that an encounter can always be described from either of two sides. The essential question, however, is on which side we should locate the real activity that brings about the encounter. In our view, this activity is assigned beyond doubt to the soul.

From a more mechanical point of view, for instance, in Muller's law of specific sense energies, it is, of course, the other way around.[43] Here the soul is seen rather as a passive apparatus in which certain stimuli, such as vibrations, chemical reactions, electromagnetic tensions, and the like, give rise to perceptions. One cannot deny that such exterior stimuli exist; we only wish to make a clear distinction between them and that which lives in them. The vibrations of the ether, or whatever the stimuli may be, are not the element leading to perception itself. This element is found in the qualities we perceive as light, color, tone, sound, taste, etc. These qualities of the universe, or essential characteristics, as we have called them, merely make use of the vibrations and stimuli in order to find their way to the soul. What are perceived in the soul, however, are the qualities themselves, which can be recognized through the inner relatedness of soul and world. This means that the world reveals itself in the form of percepts to the soul. These percepts, however, are given form by the activity of the soul. The *perceiving soul makes into pictures the qualities that the world spreads out around it.*

The closer the accord between these qualities and the percepts formed in the soul, the truer the perception. A continuous correction takes place through the ever-changing relationship between soul and world, whereby the truth of the world reveals itself to the soul in different ways and thus can be increasingly recognized. If these perceptions are to be as true as possible, the realm of the senses has to be free from disturbing elements in the soul, from the feelings and desires, emotions and affections, passions and the like, which cause false perceptions if they penetrate into the realm of the senses.

The human eye, which is completely translucent, is an example of an ideal sense-organ. The crystal clarity of the front part of the eye allows light to enter unhindered. On its way through the cornea, lens, and vitreous humor, light meets no resistance. The whole sense-sphere should be in this state of clarity in order to give rise to pure perceptions.

Feelings, desires, and other soul-forces must come to rest at the border of this sense-sphere, so that a state of balance between soul and world can be brought about.

Sense and Sense-Organ; The World Sense; The "I" and Perceiving

In our further observations we must make a distinction between sense and sense-organ. The ability of the soul to arrive at certain perceptions is what we regard as a sense; a sense-organ is then the bodily apparatus involved. Hence, we speak of a sense of sight, a sense of hearing, and the like, just as in ordinary usage. Ordinary usage also brings out the various ways in which the word "sense" is related to other faculties of the soul, over and above its reference to sense-perception. Through its derivatives, "sensuous" and "sensual," it is related to pleasurable feelings and desires. Through "sensible" and "senseless" it is related to judgments; and it is related to cognition when we speak of "making sense" of something, or of working out the "sense" of an obscure piece of writing.

These examples show that in ordinary experience the word "sense" calls up a variety of mental images. Here we touch one of the most elementary faculties of the soul—its ability to make contact with the world, to turn towards the world. On the one hand, a main characteristic of the soul is that it is always in inner movement, through which it is active in thinking, feeling, and willing. On the other hand, it is an equally essential characteristic of the soul that where this movement is brought to rest, the world-contents can express themselves in the soul and be perceived. We can therefore speak of a general "world sense" in the soul, divided into a number of special senses of which we will speak shortly.

The movement of the soul by which growth and development become possible, and by which the relationship with the world comes about, are therefore met by an inner power to withhold these movements, to bring them to rest, through which the soul takes the place of the contents of the world. This means that when the movement within is quieted, the soul as a whole becomes *sense*. The soul itself, then consisting of the qualities and essential constituents of the world that are involuted into the soul, can unite itself in a state of rest with these qualities.

The power to quiet the inner movement of the soul lies in the "I," the kernel of the whole human personality. Only where this "I" has banished all hindering soul elements from the sphere of the senses, and so has calmed this sphere entirely, can true perceiving really take place. The contents of the world reveal themselves in the sense-organs and are formed by the perceiving soul into pictures. The "I" then stands face to face with these pictures.

The Twelve Senses (Steiner)

The soul is able to relate itself to the world through its ability to perceive. A number of organs makes this possible. Opinions have changed in the course of time as to how many senses there are. Besides the original five—sight, hearing, smell, taste, and touch—senses of warmth, balance, and movement are now generally accepted. Steiner distinguished twelve senses: touch, life, movement, and balance; smell, taste, sight, and warmth; hearing, speech, thought, and "I."[44] The first four enable man to perceive how his bodily organism relates to the surrounding world. In relation to the soul this organism is "world" and is perceived as such.

The sense of touch rightly stands at the head of the list, for it is the most elementary sense that the soul has. Through the sense of touch, man distinguishes himself from his surroundings as a bodily being. This sense has such fundamental significance for the human soul that one is even inclined to ascribe an element of touch to all the other senses. All perceiving can be regarded as a touching of the soul. The sense of touch could be described as the first indication of the soul's capacity to unite with the world by means of an inner movement that is directed outwards. All other senses would then seem to be modifications of the sense of touch.

By the sense of life we mean the ability to perceive the extent to which the organism is in a state of well-being. The human organism is not only a thing in the world but is at the same time a growing, developing entity. It carries within itself the sum of life-functions related to the organ-processes. If these life-functions can develop undisturbed, in harmony with one another, they give the human soul a feeling that is carried and supported by the life-forces. Just as the sense of touch, in the narrow meaning of the word, gives the soul the feeling of being carried by the physical apparatus of the organism, so the sense of life provides this feeling in relation to the sum of the life-processes.

The sense of movement is the ability to perceive how the body, and particularly the limbs, is at rest or in movement. It does not refer, therefore, to movements outside us but to the movement of our own bodies.

The sense of balance enables a person to perceive the state of balance of his whole organism in relation to the world of space. These four senses belong together in so far as they are hidden relatively deeply in the unconscious life of the soul, leading to conscious perceptions only if some resistance or disturbance occurs. They are of the utmost importance for the whole bodily and vital existence of man, but in the conscious soul-life they play but a minor role. With the exception of the sense of touch, conscious perception of these senses is an indication of a direct threat to bodily and vital existence.

The next four senses, of smell, taste, sight, and warmth, provide direct perceptions of certain qualities in the world important for the inner life of the soul. The sense of smell is the closest to the first group, having the strongest connection with the unconscious soul-life. Certain perceptions of smell can raise memories one had thought lost, until suddenly they rise out of the darkness of the unconscious. In

80

ordinary life, people can be strongly influenced by certain smells without being conscious of it. A certain environment, a room, a house, or a city may be sympathetic or antipathetic to someone because of its smell, though he may not be aware of it. This effect also plays a greater role in human relationships than is generally supposed.

While the sense of smell leads to perceptions in an airy or gaseous medium, the sense of taste introduces a liquid element. We can taste something only when it is dissolved.

The sense of sight brings the soul into contact with the phenomena of light and color in the world; eye-muscles control the eye-movements whereby we can perceive lines, forms, and exterior movements. The eye follows any external form or movement on which it is focused, and it copies it with movements of its own. With this visual sense we reach an entirely conscious area. Our exact sciences are very largely based on the sense of sight. In the unconscious life of the soul we first meet the sense of touch; the conscious sense of sight is an ability to touch on a higher level.

The sense of warmth is of the utmost importance for the life of the human soul, and especially for the unfolding of the more spiritual functions. A certain degree of warmth in the organism is required for the soul and spirit to unfold in the human personality.

The last four senses enable the soul to penetrate into the more inward aspects of beings and phenomena. The sense of hearing enables us to perceive sounds in such a way that lifeless things and living beings come into contact with each other. In the same way, sound and tone are the means by which the subjective life of human beings and animals can be communicated perceptibly to others.

Besides the sense of hearing, we distinguish the sense of the word, or sense of speech, because the perception of a word is essentially different from the perception of a number of sounds. A word is a whole, which is indeed expressed by means of a number of sounds, but which in its essence goes beyond them. When a child learns to speak, he does so not by putting together a series of sounds but through an entire word-picture, which he learns to form in connection with things around him and his own inner feelings. By the sense of speech, therefore, we mean the ability to perceive words as such.

In addition to the sense of speech, we distinguish the sense of thought or the conceptual sense. The content of a thought is something that extends as much beyond words as words extend beyond sounds. What Goethe described as "idea," e.g., as the idea of the archetypal plant, is a spiritual reality existing on its own account and is perceived as such. The Dutch language has the beautiful word *denk-beeld* (thought-picture, or idea), which indicates how a thought appears to us as a picture. Such a picture is directly perceived by the soul.

The last in this group of twelve senses is the Ego-sense, or the sense of the "I," which means the capacity to perceive the "I" of another person and hence his spiritual being, his personality. One might suppose that here we are concerned not with a particular sense but with a very complex process. In reality, however, this is not the case, for one perceives at first the whole being of a person as his personal revelation and only later does one bring other percepts, feelings, mental images, etc. into the picture. But this sense of the "I"—like the senses of thought and speech—is very little developed in contemporary man, and its functioning, therefore, remains essentially unconscious.

The Twelve Sense Capacities

Steiner grouped these twelve senses in various ways, for example, as "inner," "outer-inner," and "outer." He also placed in one group those senses belonging to the life of the will or desire (senses of touch, life, movement, and balance);

in another group those connected with the feeling-life (senses of smell, taste, sight, and warmth); and in the third group those relating to the conceptual life (sense of hearing, speech, thought, and "I"). The importance of such groupings is to show that the senses put us in touch with various inner and outer areas, and that the degree to which impressions from the several senses enter into consciousness varies widely. In one of the notes to his book, *Von Seelenrätseln* (Riddles of the Soul, published in English as *The Case for Anthroposophy*), Steiner spoke about intentional relationships in connection with the theory of the senses.[45] He showed that we are not sufficiently aware that a person never receives an impression from one sense alone but always from several together.

Certainly the impression from one sense will rise more clearly into the foreground of consciousness while the other impressions remain dim, but the soul will thereby relate itself in more than one way to the world. Through the perceptions that come from the senses of balance, movement, life, and also the sense of touch, a man has a dimly conscious experience of his own being. If we see an object we will have, besides the vivid impression, a less conscious impression from our sense of balance, the posture of our head and body. We thus not only receive a certain idea of what we see, but at the same time we experience, though less consciously, the fact that *what we see exists also, because the experience of our own being is bound up with it.*

An experience generally will include even more layers. Perceiving a speaking person, for example, draws on the "I" sense, the senses of thought, speech, and hearing, and the sense of sight. At the same time, we experience our own being by means of the unconscious senses. As a result, we experience the reality of the speaking person as strongly as our own.

Since the twelve senses enable us to experience all the

possibilities of perception, as Steiner said, and since we are related through them to our own being as well as to the world, we find in such a theory an important means of understanding the intentional relationship between soul and world.

IV. The Development of the Soul between "I" and "World"

Polarity, Enhancement, and Metamorphosis

We can never understand the soul without seeing it as a living, developing whole. We are always dealing with an event, an inner process, because all the elements, functions, and capacities of the soul are real forces continually having evident effects. The soul, therefore, can be regarded as a stage on which a continuous drama unfolds. Its most important characteristic is the conflict between the various forces engaged in it. On this battlefield of the soul, everything aims at maintaining to the utmost its own position. The desires, the feelings, the judgments, the mental images: all lay claim to sole possession of the soul.

The reason for this conflict is the drive for development, already described, which can be regarded as one of the main characteristics of the soul. To understand this development, we must study its basic laws, laws of polarity, enhancement, and metamorphosis. We have already spoken of polarity as a dominant law in the life of the soul. The entire soul is exposed to numerous polar relationships, of which the most important is the polarity between the surrounding world and the spiritual kernel of the personality revealed in the soul. Between these two poles exists the soul-life, and forces continuously stream from inside outwards as well as the other way around. The soul is the field where "I" and "world" meet each other and where an attempt is made to build a relationship between them, a relationship that is always changing, at all times of the day as well as in every period of life.

Goethe described the law of polarity as one of the fundamental laws of all life-development, or a "rising" caused by

85

an inner urge for unfolding. It would not contradict Goethe's view if we were to describe enhancement as "spiritualization," for in his *Metamorphosis of Plants* Goethe spoke of an ascent "as on a spiritual ladder" when characterizing regular metamorphosis.[46]

What causes this development? While polarity is related to the position of the soul between "I" and world, development has its origin in the character of the "I" itself. The spiritual kernel of the personality has incarnated for its life on earth and has brought with it the great relationships with the universe, which surround it as the soul. This makes possible the relationship between "I" and world. If the "I" were not surrounded by such a personalized system of cosmic forces, it would have no possibility of experiencing its relationship with the world. The "I" would be imprisoned, so to speak, in a dark dungeon. One could say that, on the one hand, a link with the universe is broken when the "I" leaves its spiritual home at birth; on the other hand, the "I" has brought with it on its way to earthly incarnation so many of the spiritual relationships in the universe that a new relationship becomes possible. It is the force of the "I" in the soul that impels man to develop inwardly in such a way that this new relationship becomes more and more nearly complete. At the moment of death, when the "I" frees itself from the corporeal link, its journey back to the spiritual begins.

From out of a spiritual existence, the spiritual personality came to earth. Enveloped by soul-forces, it united with the body in order to go through a series of developmental phases, impelled by an inner drive to return to the spiritual world after having enriched itself with the experiences of a life on earth. In this context, the word "development" acquires profound meaning. When the spiritual personality is born, it is enclosed within several sheaths. The outermost sheath is the human body. Next to it comes the whole system of life-processes and organic functions. The most

86

intimate sheath, in closest connection with the spiritual personality, is the human soul.

The development of the soul has, therefore, the aim of enabling the "I" to liberate itself from all earthly bonds: the soul becomes an organ for the "I." At the opposite pole is the soul's inclination to become an organ for bodily life on earth. Both poles are necessary for healthy development. If the personality follows too quickly the drive to liberate itself from the earthly link, this becomes a flight from the battle that must be faced by every human being on earth. There is also the danger that the battle would be avoided by the personality remaining too connected to the physical body. Every phase of life demands a different attitude, and a new balance has to be struck again and again.

If we study the development of the soul according to the laws of polarity and enhancement, we also come to know a third law described by Goethe as the law of metamorphosis in relation to all living beings. Metamorphosis is a transformation, not a change in the usual sense of the word. If we cut off a piece of a plant, its form is changed. Metamorphosis, however, indicates a change caused by the forces at work in the inner being: "life-forces" in the plant, the force of the "I" in the soul. It is characteristic of metamorphosis that every new state is achieved by wrestling with the old one. Goethe described this type of development in his studies of the metamorphosis of plants, through which it became clear that the archetypal form of every plant, the leaf, reveals itself in a succession of developmental phases having the character of an ascent. Goethe gave expression to this principle of metamorphosis in his poem, "*Selige Sehnsucht*," in the frequently quoted words, "*Stirb und werde*" ("Die and become").

The same concept was known in ancient Greece, where it was expressed by Heraclitus, among others, in his reflections on death and birth. In his view, the little child dies so that an older self can be born; the older child dies in the adolescent, the adolescent in the man, the man in the old man. Every new stage of development emerges only if the previous stage disappears. In every metamorphosis, therefore, we have to do with a trinity consisting of the old stage, the emerging new stage, and, in between, a process of dying and becoming. In the plant, the old and the new stages are visible at the same time. One can see on the stem the first sprout as well as the leaves of the stem and sometimes also the petals of the flower. The process itself is invisible; it exists supersensibly, between the successive visible stages.

It is different with the human being. In human beings, the process between stages can be discerned. At any given time in his life, a man carries his past, as well as his future, invisibly within him. He always represents a state of becoming in which past and future are dynamically present. The adult and the old man already slumber in the child; the adult and the child still dream in the old man.

Since the various stages of form become spatially visible in the plant, one after another, its forms are essentially fixed in space, out of the stream of time, even if only for limited periods. With human beings, we cannot speak of any such fixed state but of development always proceeding in the stream of time. Having become a form in space, man is always in the process of change and metamorphosis. The various phases of human development are woven into one another. The only part having a continuous existence through all these phases, without a pause, is the kernel of the spiritual and moral personality, the "I."

Horizontal and Vertical Directions of Development

The stage where this development takes place is the human soul, and we can distinguish two main directions of development, vertical and horizontal. We have compared the vertical direction of development with a process of awakening, the horizontal with a breathing process. The vertical direction of development has two components, an

88

ascending direction from below upwards and a descending one from above downwards. The horizontal direction relates to both. The ascending development includes everything having to do with the awakening of the soul caused by natural growth and the unfolding of life. The small child literally "wakes up" by degrees. During his first phase of life, he sleeps almost continuously, carrying on his various life-functions while nearly asleep. Gradually he discovers more and more in relation to his immediate surroundings, his own bodily existence, other people, and so on.

A child's development takes place primarily in three stages: from birth until the change of teeth, from the change of teeth until puberty, and from puberty until adulthood. Each of these periods can be divided again into a number of other periods. There is, for example, a period from birth until the third year, which has a distinct inner unity. The fifth, ninth, and twelfth years are also important transition-points.

The rising direction of this development is especially visible in the small child, in whom the soul truly rises out of unconsciousness; it awakes out of the state of sleeping, which is bound up with bodily processes. Gradually a growing consciousness of the surrounding world emerges. The awakening is accompanied by an unfolding. The plant, too, not only grows upwards out of the dark earth towards the light but also expands laterally. The same process takes place in the natural development of the soul.

Gradually a relationship to the world is created. The soul builds up a picture of the world composed of experiences and perceptions. Other people are included in this world-picture. This development can be illustrated schematically with a diagram (see next page). This natural development comes to a certain conclusion around the twenty-eighth year. Up to this time, the development of body and soul proceed more or less hand in hand. During the first periods of a child's development this is entirely so; towards the end

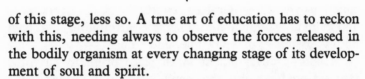

of this stage, less so. A true art of education has to reckon with this, needing always to observe the forces released in the bodily organism at every changing stage of its development of soul and spirit.

The force causing this vertically rising and horizontally expanding process of development is the force of the "I." It works from out of the hidden bodily processes and liberates itself more and more from them. Of an entirely different nature is the direction of development working into the soul from above. It originates in the relationship of the "I" to the world, in so far as this is consciously experienced in the soul. This direction of development also unites with a horizontal direction, not in the sense of an expansion into the surrounding world, as in the previous case, but now in such a way that percepts and experiences from the world are integrated.

This form of development is indicated schematically in the diagram below.

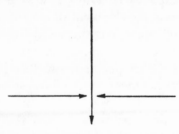

It can be seen as an awakening of the soul in its relationship to the *spiritual* universe, whereas the previously mentioned

90

development was an awakening of the soul in its relationship to the *natural* world.

This spiritual development takes place primarily after the twenty-eighth year, when natural development has reached a certain conclusion, but it can begin much earlier. Many young people, especially after the years of puberty, feel a need to concern themselves with the problems of this development. While it is the task of the art of education to foster natural development, spiritual development depends on self-education. Anyone failing to take hold of this self-education will not progress in his inner life. However important a position he may achieve in the outer world, the state of his soul will not alter much.

We must study the relationship between soul and spirit in order to get to know the laws which are at work here. In this connection Scheler mentioned a number of significant viewpoints. He indicated the force that enables man to overcome the natural existence in which the animal is entirely absorbed: "The animal lives entirely in the concrete and in reality. A point in space and time is connected with every reality, a here and a now, as given by sense-perception from a certain aspect. To be a man means to hurl a strong 'No' at this reality."[48] This can be done only out of the spirit.

In connection with our earlier considerations, we must conclude: the spirit within ourselves, the spirit revealing itself in the soul as an active force, is the "I." In the "I" we find the dynamic principle wherein the whole development of the soul is rooted.

The Path of Self-Development; Knowledge of the
World and Self-Knowledge

One deals in this development with a spiritualization of the natural forces arising in the human soul. The "I," coming to know through its connection with the spiritual universe the three great ideals of truth, beauty, and goodness,

91

strives to apply them as a measure for everything that comes to conscious life through judging and forming mental images and in the experience of pleasure and displeasure, sympathy and antipathy, craving and desire.

The path to this goal has been illuminated by all religions, by all great mystics and spiritual philosophers. For modern times, Steiner's approach to inner schooling by means of spiritual science offers a practical path that is fully conscious and rests on sound epistemological foundations. This path is based on the realization that the human being not only can gain conscious awareness of the kind of forces at work in his soul but is also capable of transforming these forces. For this purpose, it is necessary that he learn to experience and to know the universe as well as the deeper being of himself.

Knowledge of the universe and self-knowledge are both necessary for modern man; they are two paths to the same goal. Steiner began by pointing to the power of reverence, reverence towards everything that reveals itself as true, good, and beautiful. Man must make it his task to observe the surrounding world in such a way that this power of reverence becomes more and more strongly alive in his soul. In this way the soul learns to open itself fully to everything revealing itself in the spiritual existence of the universe. The soul, therefore, consciously strives to open itself to the highest revelations of the surrounding world, and these revelations can speak to the human soul because they come from the wisdom, beauty, and goodness of the natural and spiritual world order. They express themselves in the striving towards high ideals of the most outstanding representatives of mankind, in the three areas of wisdom, beauty, and morality.

While the soul must work to open itself entirely to the highest forces working in the world, it is equally necessary for it to become consciously aware of its own inner being. For this, one practices an inner calmness through which all the restlessness brought about by ordinary life is silenced.

The soul has to set itself at an inner distance from everything with which it is usually occupied. For anyone who can observe himself in this, it is like looking from a high mountain peak at the landscape far below, and in this way coming to know how the two levels are related.

This objective observer can become increasingly the higher man within ourselves; that is, he can identify himself increasingly with the spiritual-moral kernel of the personality, the "I." This "I" can *become* the guide of the inner soul-life, but only if a person has learned in this way to distinguish his "I" from the egohood that is in ordinary life the center of the soul forces.

There is a strange and profound connection between these two paths that lead respectively to the world and to the true "I." The connection is expressed in Steiner's words:

> If man fully knows himself,
> His self becomes the world;
> If man fully knows the world,
> The world becomes his self.[49]

In other words, through organizing knowledge of the universe, man reaches true self-knowledge, and through practicing true self-knowledge he comes to know the world. This relationship is comprehensible if we remember what was said earlier about the relationship of man and world, of the human soul and the world soul: they are intimately related. Both are composed of the same spiritual substance; they belong together like microcosm and macrocosm, as was said in earlier centuries. The involuted world soul shows itself in the inner life of man; the human soul turned outwards reveals itself in the essential qualities of the universe.

When one has practiced the first two stages of this path, the systematic work of the "I" begins on the forces active in the soul. The aim is to give these forces their proper place between "I" and world and to develop and strengthen them. Desiring, feeling, and forming mental images especially, must be freed from their subjective links and personal, arbitrary actions. Through various groups of systematically designed exercises, a person going through such a schooling can learn to build his mental images out of the wisdom that speaks in the universe. He will learn to penetrate his desires with the deepest moral forces that can unfold in man's "I" and to bring his feelings into harmony with the real love streaming between "I" and world. In this way, the three archetypal forces of thinking, feeling, and willing can come to full development in the soul.

The Dynamic Character of Soul-Life

Once again we wish to emphasize the dynamic character of the entire soul-life. Everything in it must be regarded as following a long path of development in which everything is fluid, continually moving and changing. In this great path of development, the soul's whole process of becoming is guided in two directions: towards an awakening of the natural man, who rises out of the obscurity of bodily processes to unfold in the expanse of the universe, and towards spiritualization, whereby the soul carries the wisdom of the universe into the life of the soul.

On one side is the force of desiring, through which the soul is embedded into the processes and functions of the organs of the living body; on the other side is the force of cognition, as the highest soul-function, unfolding where the spirit penetrates the soul.

Carus pointed to the important relationship between the bodily process of propagation, which is directly linked with desires, and the process of cognition.[50] The German *erkennen* (to know, to cognize, to recognize) evolves out of *arkannjan*, in which one can find the root *kunni*, which means creation, or copulation. The German translation of the Bible uses the phrase *"ein Weib erkennen"* ("to know a woman," meaning the act of physical union). A similar relationship appears

94

also in the Latin *noscere*, to know, and *nasci*, to be born, and in the French *connnaitre* and *naitre*. (Publisher's note: The same relationship between cognition and reproduction exists in the English language: a woman conceives and an idea is conceived; in some English translations of the Old Testament the phrase "to know a woman" is used repeatedly.) Here also the wisdom of the spirit of language gives insights into original relationships that have lapsed from ordinary consciousness.

V. Consciousness

THE DEVELOPMENT OF CONSCIOUSNESS

Consciousness as a Condition in which the Soul Finds Itself

Until now we have not spoken about consciousness but have taken it for granted that the soul has knowledge of itself through consciousness. We must not, as often happens, equate consciousness with the soul, with either the whole soul-life or the content of the soul. We have regarded the soul as a being that exists, resting in itself, as a spiritual reality related to the whole universe and its phenomena and yet also independent.

When we speak about consciousness, we mean nothing but a particular condition in which the soul finds itself. One often encounters the view that consciousness is the real object of psychology, that psychology could become an exact science, because the concept of consciousness is clearly defined. From our observations there can be no other object in psychology than the soul itself, with all its changing content.

The Dutch word for consciousness, *bewustzijn* (German *Bewusstsein*), shows that we are dealing with a state of "being" (*zijn*, *sein*), which is determined by a "knowing" (*weten*, *wissen*), an inner knowing. In the Dutch verb *begrijpen*, German *begreifen* (to comprehend), the prefix "be" indicates an internalization of *grijpen* or *greifen* (grasping); this is also the case with the word *bewustzijn*, in which we are concerned not with a knowing of something external but a knowing that is directed inward. When we know that the sky is cloudy, for example, this need not touch us inwardly any further. If we are conscious of knowing it, this means that the knowing has an inner significance for us. In this connection we may also note the German *Gewissen* (conscience), of which the main word is *Wissen* (knowing). The prefix *"ge"* points to the past in such a way that *Gewissen* expresses something that rises in the soul as knowledge from the past.

Self-Consciousness; Different States of Consciousness

The knowing that lives in our soul is consciousness. Consciousness can relate to the world in which the soul is living as well as to the knowing that arises in the soul itself. In the latter case, we have a knowing about knowing; consciousness then becomes self-consciousness and, eventually, an "I"-consciousness. Knowing that relates to the world embraces not only so-called external phenomena but also one's own body and bodily processes, which for the experiencing soul belong to the outer world as much as to the feelings, emotions, and other experiences that arise in the soul.

Consciousness, therefore, is a condition of soul characterized by knowledge of what reveals itself in and through the soul, of what comes from the outer world or from the inner world of the soul. It follows that consciousness can unfold in various ways and directions. It may be limited and narrow, wide and comprehensive, profound or superficial. Consciousness develops to a certain stage through experience of life itself, embracing more and more objects as its range of interests expands. Through sorrows and painful experiences, consciousness is deepened. In science and art, and in religious-ethical life, a widening and deepening of consciousness can be achieved.

Bodily Development and the Development of Consciousness; The Mistake of Materialism

Consciousness as a state of being is characterized by knowing. It depends upon the capacity of cognition, which is an ability of the soul, as is the ability to experience. If we wish to penetrate the secret of consciousness, however, we

97

must recognize a fact hardly recognized by present-day psychology, that everything appearing in the human being as life-forces is in polar opposition to everything connected with consciousness. *Life and consciousness are in opposition.*

We noted this opposition in another connection when we discussed feelings, remarking that the positive feelings (pleasure, joy, sympathy) are related to the stream of life-forces revealing themselves in the life-processes. In considering the soul's capacity to experience, we learned of a state in which the soul unites again with the universe, in other words, in which it is permeated by those forces from the universe that serve life's unfolding.

In contrast, we spoke of the negative feelings (displeasure, pain, antipathy) in connection with an inclination on the part of the soul to withdraw from the universe, to shut itself off from those forces experienced as serving life's unfolding. This last process makes possible the cognizing functions of the soul (forming judgments and mental images).

To be absolutely precise, one should say that a separation of the soul from the universe begins with the first experience of the simplest, most elementary sensations and feelings. Even here, the soul retains something for itself. It does not immerse itself in the stream of life. The beginning of this process of isolation has therefore to be sought in the soul's past experiences. The process, however, develops further when negative feelings arise, and, as a result, judgment and forming mental images become possible. The soul then withdraws entirely from the stream of life-forces and opposes them in cognition, establishing the basis for the emergence of consciousness.

There is always a tendency to imagine that life and consciousness develop side by side, or parallel to one another. We see, for example, how a child grows and develops physically, passing through a number of stages, marked by the changing of teeth, puberty, and the like. It is easy to assume that the development of consciousness follows a corresponding path. In fact, just the opposite is the case. Here we must observe not one direction of development but two directions. Bodily development contrasts with the development of consciousness, which is more a reverse development, or, as Steiner put it, a "de-development."

Space is made free for consciousness precisely when bodily development is withheld. Evolution in the field of life means unfolding organic processes whereby the body is kept alive and propagates itself. Involution in the field of life is the first necessary condition for spiritual development based on consciousness. Steiner expressed this in the following words:

> Life sprouts and blossoms, but into this sprouting and blossoming life there comes a continual disintegration. Life disintegrates continually within us. The sprouting, blossoming life is giving way all the time to disintegration. We really die partially at every moment; something within us disintegrates. We can only build it up again and again. But if something disintegrates within us materially, the soul-spiritual has room to penetrate us, to be active within us. Here we meet the great error of materialism. Materialism assumes that the sprouting, blossoming life develops upwards in man, up into the nerves, and that just as the muscles are built up out of the blood, so are the nerves, as indeed they are. But thinking does not develop as a result of the nerves being built up; neither does feeling. On the contrary, it is because the nerves disintegrate in a certain sense, as though pierced by holes, that the soul-spiritual slips into this disintegration. We must first break down the material; only then can the soul-spiritual appear in us and we are enabled to experience it ourselves.[51]

99

Capacities for Regeneration in Plants and in the Soul

We can study in nature the extent to which the life-forces diminish with the development of consciousness. In the plant world we find an unlimited capacity for regeneration. However much one may prune trees and bushes, new branches will sprout again close to the old ones. This capacity for regeneration is still present in the lower animals; in the higher animals it vanishes. It is least developed in man, especially since he has evolved beyond the tribal stage. It is remarkable, however, that we again find this capacity for regeneration in the human soul, in the field of memories, mental images, and thoughts. What the plant is able to do with its branches and leaves, namely to reproduce everything that has been lost, man can do with his memories, mental images, and thoughts. From a few fragments, we can bring to mind a whole memory-picture. Modern *Gestalt* psychology has shown how this impulse always to produce a whole exists in the forming of mental images and thoughts and works there as a primary force. We could speak here of a metamorphosis by which a certain force that always brings about a whole in organic life now takes hold of part of the soul in order to do the same for the cognizing functions.

The Polarity between Life and Consciousness

The idea of polarity between life and consciousness has been fully developed only by Steiner. In countless lectures and writings he drew attention to this point. He did have a predecessor in this field, however; Karl Fortlage, a psychologist in the second half of the nineteenth century, who earned immortality for this idea alone.[52] In Fortlage's treatise, "On the Nature of the Soul," he discussed the relationship between life and consciousness: "Consciousness belongs to those nature-processes which through their very existence consume the force whereby they exist." "Consciousness is the destroying principle of life, the surplus of consumption over nourishment, and, therefore, a direct path to death."

"Only in so far as we sleep do we live; when we wake, we begin to die." "This positive death, in which the activity of questioning is at home, is not a mere negation of life but an all-consuming power." These profound and beautiful thoughts reach their conclusion in the sentence: "Consciousness is a small and partial death; death is a great and total consciousness, an awakening of the entire being in its innermost depths."

Life and Death in Minerals, Plants, and Animals in Comparison to Man

Out of the opposition between life and consciousness rises the question of the deeper relationship between consciousness and death. Fortlage's remark that we really live only when we sleep and begin to die when we wake opens magnificent views regarding this question, enabling us to penetrate more deeply into the psychological meaning of the nature of death. How is death related—or how, indeed, are life and death related—to the development of the soul? We will first examine these relationships in nature. Normally we apply the words life and death in the same sense to all the kingdoms of nature. We speak of a living plant, a living animal, a living man. What is not living we call dead. We speak of the mineral world as inanimate and contrast it with the animate. Plant, animal, and man are dead for us when life has gone from them.

If we wish to understand the terms "life" and "death" in a deeper sense, such a generalized use of these words is not permissible. In what respect can we regard this so-called "inanimate" nature as dead? Does the term "death" stand here in opposition to the term "life"? No, the minerals, stones, metals, and crystals cannot be regarded as dead in this sense. Their mode of existence is not the opposite of being alive. From this point of view, they are neither dead nor alive. They *are*. They are as little subject to life and death as are the stars in the heavens above. Crystals have their geometric forms, their inner light, and their colors as an expression of forces that point to the relationship between earth and universe through the centuries.

We do indeed find, during the long periods of earth-development, a coming and going in the minerals, a becoming and vanishing, but this process is only remotely comparable with what we know in earthly life as birth and death.

We must look at the plant world in order to meet life as such. Plant life develops through the seasons and depends upon seasonal changes. Annual plants appear in spring and come to full flower in summer, together with all the green vegetation; in autumn and winter they fade away. Here we see life expressed in thousands of forms and colors, and at a later season we see it disappear again. Plant life keeps in step with the rhythm of the seasons, passing through a series of stages in endless metamorphosis. The laws of life itself, the laws of the organic world, are revealed here. Goethe tried to define these laws with his concepts of polarity and enhancement. The whole plant world, in its continuous metamorphosis of the leaf, shows an uninterrupted sequence of the stages of life. This is the appearance of life itself.

What we call "death" in the plant, the withering away, is nothing but a receding development in which the same laws of metamorphosis are valid. From leaf to blossom, from blossom to pistil, from pistil to seed, from seed to sprout: it is all an uninterrupted sequence of manifestations of the eternal life-force that rules the plant world.

In Goethe's work, *The Metamorphosis of Plants*, there is an unusual chapter in which he speaks about Schelver, who firmly refused to submit to the idea of bisexual propagation of plants.[53] Although Goethe did not go as far as Schelver, he regarded his ideas as highly significant. To Goethe himself, the "eternal marriages" in the plant world were antipathetic. He could not bring the notion of sexual propagation of the plant into harmony with his idea of metamorphosis.

For him, it is characteristic of the plant that it takes root in the moist earth, finds its way up into the sphere of air, light, and warmth, and finally produces seed out of the same inner force that dominates the whole process of metamorphosis. Thus the life of the plants proceeds perpetually from one stage of existence to another, always leaving behind a process of fading and withering. Whereas in the mineral world we find a state beyond life and death, or below life and death, in the plant world we meet life itself.

To know death we must turn our gaze to the animal kingdom. The animals, too, are born in a stream of life, working in the groups and species through the force of heredity. The animal, however, cannot unfold its life unhindered, as the plant can. Another stream of forces enters the being of the animal and permeates it. Capacities arise which, in this form at least, are unknown in the plant world: sense-perceptions with inwardly experienced reaction, the possibility of free movement over the earth and all that goes with it. While the plant lives entirely in its outer unfolding of life, something from this stream of forces is withheld in the animal and used for the inner life of the soul. It is as though these forces must be wrested from the natural process of life. Death thus appears in the animal kingdom. A certain state of consciousness arises and binds the animal to the inner forces characteristic of every animal species.

Each species of animals represents a certain group of inner qualities in which the animal is imprisoned. The essence of the wolf is defined by its forces of desire; they not only determine his inner state but shape his whole outer form. Each species of animal has a form, image, and finally a whole bodily construction that are the immediate expression of the drives and desires living in it. The animal, therefore, is fixed in a certain state of existence by the death forces working in it, from which it cannot free itself. On the one side are the life-forces that stream through every animal species and are the source from which new examples arise

103

again and again. On the other side, each example is directly determined by its inner nature. The wolf remains a wolf, and it is a better representative of its species the more completely it carries the complex of desires characteristic of its whole nature.

After the animal has reached maturity, no further development occurs, at least not in the sense that new capacities can be developed out of the animal itself. The chicken that slips out of the egg has nearly the same capabilities as the mature hen, except for not being able to lay eggs. When the chicken is able to do this, it has nearly reached the end of its development. How many years it lives after that has almost no bearing on the development of its inner being. One could say that, from the time of its maturity onwards, every animal has something like the characteristics of the old animal, in the sense that with maturity it has reached its final stage of development. This is the tragedy residing in an animal that a sensitive person feels unconsciously: the irrevocable bondage to its one-sided and limited complex of instincts and drives. Hence the outer form of every animal has an element of caricature, caused by the one-sided limitation it expresses.

The forces of death, which are connected with consciousness, appear in quite a different way in man. The animal is caught in the grip of death from the moment of its birth, and especially from its maturity onward. Of man we cannot say that he is unable to develop himself further once he has reached adulthood. The opposite is true. When man has reached a certain maturity through the life-forces that determine his natural existence, space becomes free for his *real human development*, which offers unlimited possibilities. If a man is twenty, forty, or sixty years old, entirely new possibilities can open in his soul, and immense inner changes can be made. The more he is "man," the more evident this process will be.

Thus the forces of death that form the basis of consciousness do not imprison man in their grip but give him the opportunity for a progressive development of his inner being. This is what Fortlage probably meant when he spoke of "positive death."

In the animal, death is a negative force only; it has the general effect of limiting and hardening organic life. In the human being, real development takes place on the basis of and through two forces. Life and death are both positive: their polar relationship creates the possibility of an inner balance through which the eternal being of man can reveal itself in the soul.

Man and Animal; Self-Consciousness; "I"-Consciousness

In this connection one can point to the difference in consciousness between man and animal. It is the inner balance between the forces of life and death that enables the human being to unfold his consciousness in relation to his own inner being. His inner being can still depend on his bodily state, or on certain drives and desires that arise in the soul; nevertheless, man has the capacity to become conscious of his own being. Self-consciousness has arisen in this way.

The animal has no self-consciousness. Its consciousness is always directed towards things connected with the necessities of life: nutrition, propagation, protection, safety. Its consciousness is poured out into this need for the satisfaction of desires. Impelled by drives or desires, animal consciousness opens itself to a certain object and is closed again after attaining it. In other words, the animal's consciousness contains exclusively whatever speaks from outside to its desire. When the desire is satisfied, the animal sinks back into a state of sleep or dream-like consciousness.

In man, consciousness can be brought to bear on the state of his own being. Self-consciousness may arise from the experience of a certain bodily state of health, strength, or well-being, from interior states of mere rest and balance in the soul, or through knowing about certain forces or faculties within oneself. We must, however, distinguish between this self-consciousness and the state of the soul known here as "I"-consciousness. We have often spoken of the "I" as the kernel of the whole personality, and of how it can reveal itself in the soul-life. The "I"-consciousness is that state of consciousness in which total attention is directed to this kernel of the personality. We could, therefore, call this "I"-consciousness a more spiritual state of consciousness, superior to the self-consciousness more concerned with the soul and the life of the organism. Through his "I"-consciousness, man experiences how the kernel of his personality rises above the stream of life and death forces and belongs to the kingdom of eternity.

Life, Consciousness, and "I"-Consciousness

The following diagram can clarify the relationships between life, consciousness, and "I"-consciousness:

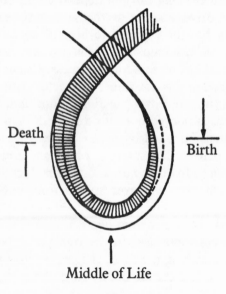

Death

Birth

Middle of Life

106

The soul, emerging from a spiritual state of existence, begins to awaken to consciousness at birth. Consciousness is initially limited to sensing certain states of the body. The soul's life is still dominated by the stream of life-forces (white band). Only around mid-life has consciousness (striped band) sufficiently unfolded that it is in a certain balance with the life-forces. Consciousness increases continuously towards the end of life, at least in a healthy development, until it permeates and surrounds the soul at the moment of death, whereby the stream of life-forces is disconnected. The "I"-consciousness awakens only gradually (broken band, continued as a black line), making it possible for man to regard life and death as phases of a single developmental process, through which his personality-kernel must work.

Habitual Actions, Embarrassment, and Consciousness

Consciousness, as a force directed against the stream of life, exerts an influence that slows down human behavior originating in the experiencing part of the soul. We wish now to draw attention to the consequences of this fact. Many human actions that originally arise from drives, desires, and feelings become habit after a time. Such actions are taken into the realm of life-processes and the nearly unconscious soul-processes directly linked with them. Great inner attention and much effort are necessary in learning to walk, speak, write, etc. After a time, all this takes place by itself, that is, without consciousness. It is a well-known phenomenon, however, that walking, standing, or writing can be difficult if one has to consider carefully *how* one does it, or if somebody else draws attention to it. In the simplest things done daily without effort, a person will suddenly become uncertain if he gives them full attention, that is, if they are taken into consciousness.

The story of the centipede who could not walk any more when he was asked with which foot he usually took the first step illustrates this humorously. The common experience of embarrassment is also sometimes connected with the slowing down of the life-functions by consciousness. Here we have to do, in the first place, with a hindering influence working from consciousness into the spontaneously acting life-forces. These life-forces can promote an uncomplicated relationship with people around one, but if consciousness works too strongly it will bind these forces, giving rise to the painful feeling we call embarrassment. This phenomenon is to a certain extent normal in the adolescent and is overcome in the right way when life and consciousness are brought increasingly into balance, so that "I"-consciousness gradually gains a place in the soul.

SLEEPING, DREAMING, AND WAKING

Conscious: Cognitive Functions (Destruction);
Unconscious: Vegetative Processes (Regeneration);
Half-Conscious: Enlivening Functions; Waking,
Sleeping, Dreaming

Superficial judgment can easily distinguish the three states of consciousness that occur in ordinary life, but great difficulties arise with closer observation. It seems at first so easy to tell whether someone is awake, dreaming, or sleeping. In reality, though, we have to do with continuous transitions. For example, observe waking consciousness more closely. The consciousness of a man awake in the ordinary way is different from the consciousness of someone solving a mathematical task or playing in a chess contest. Imagine someone walking through a quiet park in the morning after waking; he crosses a street with much traffic and then has to deal with a complicated matter in his office. Under all three conditions he is awake, but in very different ways. First he will be awake only in the sense that his eyes are open, while his soul, though indeed living in the realm of perceptual images, is still bound in large measure to the processes that dominate the organism during sleep. Next, his soul must rouse itself into greater activity in the field of perceptions and concepts, for he must decide immediately where and when to cross the street. In the third moment, his whole soul must be brought into activity. The forces of judging and thinking, as much as those of feeling and willing, all come into play.

There is a similar difference in dreams, of which we will speak later in more detail. There is a great difference between dreams during the night and so-called daydreams, and daydreams themselves are not all of one kind. In some daydreams a person may be completely lost in a memory or fantasy, while on another occasion he may merely drift into a dreamy mood while remaining quite awake. If we wish to characterize these three states of consciousness briefly, we could say: in waking the soul is active in perceiving, forming mental images, and finally thinking. Regarding sleep, we may have the impression that no single connection remains between the life-functions and the body. This is true of dreamless sleep in relation to the cognizing and experiencing functions. The soul works very strongly during sleep, however, regenerating the body. The will-life, which remains quite unconscious, is then directed to the regeneration of the processes that have been disturbed by consciousness during daily life.

In dreaming, the soul is especially active in the realm of feelings, in ways to be described later, or—to express it more completely—in all of the experiencing functions. From this it follows that we must regard the so-called waking man as often, and even most of the time, only partly awake. A great portion of the soul, in so far as it lives in the feelings, "dreams" during waking life, or even "sleeps," if the soul is given up to vegetative processes. It is customary to speak of a conscious, an unconscious, and also a subconscious soul-life. The three states of consciousness we have mentioned—waking, dreaming, sleeping—can be designated conscious, half-conscious, and unconscious. In this connection we could say that the soul is entirely unconscious of its relationship to the bodily processes and the life-forces. This unconscious soul-life is in the service of nutrition, metabolism, and propagation, in brief, everything that has to do with building up and maintaining our bodily existence.

The soul lives consciously in sense-perceptions, mental images, and thoughts. Here, therefore, the soul works in the destructive forces that form the basis of consciousness. In desires, cravings, and feelings we have to do with the half-conscious soul-life, which forms a middle realm between the two poles of the conscious and the unconscious.

Thinking, Feeling, Willing; Nerve-Sense Processes;
Rhythmical Processes (Lung, Heart); Metabolic Processes

Steiner was the first to show how the whole life of the soul relates to the three systems of organs upon which our bodily existence is built. This is not some mystical notion concerning the "seat of the soul," the kind of notion found repeatedly in modern thinking, as when someone wishes to localize the whole soul-life in the brain or in the central nervous system. Nor is it a question of an abstract psychophysical parallelism, a view found all too often in modern psychology. The thoughts described here by Steiner are among the most important thoughts that have been brought to bear on physiology and psychology in recent times. For Steiner, the soul is "localized" in the totality of bodily processes: in the brain, the central and sympathetic nerve systems, in the rhythmical processes at work in the respiration and the blood circulation, and in all those processes belonging to metabolism in the widest sense of the word. The most important point, however, is that Steiner indicated the relationship between particular soul-functions and organic processes.[54]

It is generally recognized that the bodily basis for sense-perception and the forming of mental images has to be sought in the whole nerve system together with the sense-organs. This is a field that has been carefully researched, and a broad knowledge of single phenomena pertaining to it has been obtained. It is different with the relationship that Steiner described between feeling and the rhythmic processes. The latter include not only the rhythms of respiration and blood-circulation but the peristaltic movements of the stomach and intestines, the vibrations of the muscles, the contractions of the finer blood-vessels, etc.: in short, the sum of rhythmic processes that stream through our entire organism.

Just as one can see in the brain a kind of center of all nerve processes, so can one see a center of rhythmic processes in the rhythmic organs of the chest, especially with the respiration and blood circulation linked to it. In these rhythmic processes we have the basis for our feeling-life. Steiner illustrated this relationship between feeling and forming mental images with an example. Musical experience is essentially based on feeling. The content, however, which reaches us through the music and is received through hearing, becomes a mental image within us. This mental image, which arises in connection with the ear and hearing, ought not to be confused with the musical experience itself. The latter comes about because the experiencing soul is connected not only with what is perceived and pictured but also with the breathing rhythm. This breathing rhythm transports itself through the spinal fluid and the liquid of the brain into the nerve system, or, as Steiner expressed it: "Something is released in the breathing rhythm through the fact that the neural process impinges on rhythmic life."[55]

When something is "felt," a change in the breathing rhythm occurs, by which a feeling arises in the soul. In other words, the soul lives in feeling if it connects itself with breathing in the same way as it connects itself with nerve-processes in forming mental images. The third force of the soul, willing, is connected with the metabolic system. Here, too, we must observe that metabolism is not linked only to a few organs. Just as our nerve system and rhythmic system penetrate the whole organism, so also does the metabolic system.

Consciousness in Thinking, Feeling, and Willing;
Sensory and Motor Nerves and the Metabolic Process

Clearly, the three systems also penetrate one another. A kind of metabolism is needed in the nerve system as well as a connection with the rhythmic processes. This applies also to the metabolic and rhythmic systems, but the rhythmic and metabolic processes are present to a lesser degree in the nerve-sense system. This is shown, for example, by the very low capacity of nerve-tissue to regenerate itself. The rhythmic processes and the nerve processes, on the other hand, work only weakly into the metabolic system.

The real basis for willing resides in the metabolic system, which embraces all the processes occurring between the absorption of nourishment by the walls of the intestines and its passage into the blood. The whole digestive system is a preparation for the metabolic process. It still belongs, in great part, to the nerve-sense system. Since the muscles, and especially those of the limbs, take up so much space in the metabolic process, Steiner also speaks of the "metabolic-limb system." The outer relationship of this system with willing is evident in the fact that the organs by which man brings his will into action are his limbs.

As far as a deeper relationship is concerned, we must remember that the human being is fully conscious in his soul only in his perceptions and mental images. His feelings are half-conscious, just like the breathing process, which can be influenced only to a certain extent. Willing, however, is carried out unconsciously, as is the whole metabolic process. We tend to regard this differently, because we carry in our consciousness the mental image that accompanies the will,

112

together with something of the feeling or emotion that goes hand in hand with the will. Willing itself, however, can in no way be experienced through ordinary daily consciousness.

Steiner illustrated the difference between willing and forming mental images and ideas:

> The experience of image-forming or ideation is somewhat like looking at a colored surface, while willing is like looking at a black area in the middle of a colored field. We see nothing in the uncolored part of the surface precisely because—unlike the surrounding part, from which color impressions are received —no such impressions come from it. We 'have the idea' of willing, because within the psyche's field of ideational experience a patch of non-ideation inserts itself, very much as the interruptions of consciousness brought about by sleep insert themselves into the continuum of conscious life.[56]

The threefold constitution of the human organism throws light on the question of the so-called sensory and motor nerves. Steiner developed the idea that these two kinds of nerves are essentially similar:

> The so-called motor nerve does not serve movement, as in the way supposed by the theory of two kinds of nerves, but, as a carrier of nerve-activity, it serves the inner perception of the metabolic process which is the ground of willing, just as the sensory nerve provides for perception of what takes place in the sense-organ.[57]

Such a statement seems absurd to those educated entirely in modern nerve-physiology, because they are accustomed to taking a great number of facts, based upon experiments, illness, and injuries, as proof that there are motor and sen-

113

sory nerves. One should ask oneself first, however, without prejudice, if these same facts could equally well prove something entirely different, namely, that the so-called motor nerve is responsible for perception of the metabolic process, which is directly connected with the life of the will, and thereby brings willing into connection with forming mental images. If we also realize that everything in the soul is founded on unity—that thinking, feeling, willing, and all the functions connected with them always appear in company—we can understand that action by the will is impossible if perception of the metabolic process, which belongs to the will, is missing.

The Three Organ-Systems and the Blood; Thinking, Feeling, Willing, and the "I"

The three organ-systems described above make up the whole human organism. There is exterior differentiation among these three organ-systems in that the centers of their activity are indicated respectively in the formation of the head, the chest, and the stomach and limbs. It must always be emphasized, however, that all three organ-systems are at work everywhere in the organism, even if they work with varying intensities.

The blood plays a remarkable role in relation to these three systems. It streams continuously through the whole organism and thus connects the various systems of organs with one another. One could describe the blood as a fourth system of organs making the three others into a unity. This immediately invites comparison with the role of the "I" amidst the three groups of soul-functions, in which thinking, feeling, and willing reveal themselves. Just as the mental image of the "I" accompanies all other mental images, including those of feeling and willing, so we can say that every function of a bodily organ is linked with the all-connecting, all-permeating blood process.

114

THE LANGUAGE OF DREAMS

Dreams and the Will Process; Dreams'
Illogical Character; Pictures; Drama

Rarely is the soul experienced as a supersensible reality so intensely as in dreams. Everyone who dreams is familiar with the strange feeling of experiencing something that left a much greater and deeper impression upon his soul than do the experiences of daily life. One has the feeling of having been in contact with a real world where things have a greater importance than usual for the life of the soul. This strange quality of dreams has been known throughout the ages. The fascination of a dream is that in it one meets the soul in its direct relationship to the universe, albeit concealed by a mask. The directness of the experience makes us conscious of the link with our spiritual origin.

To understand the peculiar nature of dreams, we must first describe in what way dream-life is different from conscious daily life. First of all, it is characteristic of the dream that it can be entirely illogical. Our memories and our behavior in ordinary life are bound by certain laws that our logical consciousness can grasp. This is not so in dreams. Someone can dream that he is alone in a room; while he observes this, someone else arrives in the room without having entered it. The newcomer may be an old man, but as soon as the dreamer speaks to him, the old man becomes a child, and finally the dreamer may discover that he himself is this child. The illogical nature of dreams has to do with the fact that, while our memories and behavior in ordinary life are always linked with our perceptions and mental images, which are all framed in accordance with our relationship to the world, in a dream the soul has withdrawn from this world and its conscious activities into a half-conscious state.

The second characteristic of dreams is that they run their course in a world of pictures. These pictures are "sense-

115

pictures" (*zinnebeelden*) or symbols. This picture-creating characteristic of dreams gives us insight into one of the deepest mysteries of the human being. We drew attention to the interrelationships among the forces of desire, which direct the growth, metabolism, and propagation of the human organism. Here we encounter the whole complex of forces that stream into the life-maintaining workings of the will.

These forces, ruled by the unconscious activity of the "I," build up our organs, giving them the form they need for carrying out their functions. In their totality these forces build the entire human organism, its whole form (*Gestalt*), and thereby display the picture of man himself as a personality. As man appears before us, he is the picture of the unconsciously working "I," which lives as a divine-spiritual spark in the soul. When we speak of man as a being created according to the image of God, the deeper meaning of the phrase is that the unconscious "I" lives in close relationship to the divine-spiritual forces of creation streaming through the universe. This complex of forces, which is connected with the will, can reveal itself unhindered in dreams, when the soul has lost its connection with the things that surround us during the day. The consequence is that all inner sensations, states, or tensions appear in symbolic forms; in dreams everything becomes pictorial.

The third characteristic of dreams is their tendency to drama. Our experience in dreams is above all dramatic. The reason for this is that our feelings, which live in the half-conscious nature of the soul, are no longer connected with the inner world of perception and the dominance of coherent mental images. Hence they can go their own way and develop unhindered according to their inclinations. In daily life, too, the feelings have a tendency towards dramatic development, but in most cases this tendency is restrained at a certain stage, because a correction comes from the realm of perceptions and mental images. Only when the feelings come so

116

violently into movement that the life of perceptions and mental images can no longer master them does a dramatic development take place, for example, if a mood of panic or something similar has arisen, or if the person concerned has to undergo too great a joy or too strong a pain. This state, however, exists continually in dreams.

Organ Dreams; Dreams as Wish-Fulfillment;
Dreams as Myth and Legend; Prophetic Dreams

On the basis of these three main characteristics, one can classify dreams in four groups. By far the largest number of dreams are the so-called organ dreams. These consist in a sensation from an organ being symbolized and dramatized by the dreaming soul. A man may dream, for example, that he suddenly hears a call that a fire has broken out. He will go, in his dream, to the window, look out, and see that a red glow is gathering over the city. Awakened by fear or horror, he finds that this room is warmer than usual and that his organism was thus in an unnatural state of warmth. Or there is the well-known dream in which the dreamer finds himself surrounded by snakes and manifold creeping animals, a dream possibly caused by a disturbance or overtaxing of the digestive system. The distorted processes of the stomach and intestines give rise to the picture of curling snakes. A typical dream belonging to this organ-group is the following: someone is walking in the woods when suddenly a dog jumps at him from out of the bushes and bites his arm. On waking, the dreamer finds that he has disturbed a nerve by lying on his arm, so that the arm hurts or is hindered in its movements. If the same thing were to happen in the day-time while sitting in a chair with one arm over the back, no symbolic or dramatic development would occur; one would simply notice what has happened.

Sometimes these organ dreams can be very complicated and at the same time reveal great beauty in their pictures. If a person has a harmonious and disciplined soul-life, the dramatic element is indicated more lightly in his dreams, while richness of pictures in them can be very great. The origin of such dreams can then be clearly recognized by someone who knows the real nature of organ-processes.

The second group is that of wish-fulfillment dreams, inspired by the forces arising from the life of desires, and which take on symbolic and dramatic forms. Since the life of desires is closely related to the whole complex of life-forces and hence also to the organ-processes, these wish dreams differ only slightly from organ dreams. Children's dreams have the same pattern on the whole. The child wants something and dreams that he gets it. In adults these dreams are no longer so simple. Their desires and demands are often more hidden and may be concealed from waking consciousness.

In a third group we find dreams with a more logically structured content. The pictures appear in a more coherent sequence and the dream can therefore take on the characteristics of a meaningful story or legend. The dramatic and symbolic tendency is present as strongly as in the two preceding groups. The difference is that these dreams are not evoked by any organ-disturbance or tension in the life of desires but by problems of inner development for the soul. Someone dreams, for example, at a time when his sense of duty is in conflict with a liking for artistic fantasy, that in a large garden he is occupied with loading knotted tree trunks onto a carriage drawn by black goats. He is continually disturbed in this work by a beautiful white stag; the stag tries again and again to run away and he is responsible for it. Such a dream pictures an unresolved state of the soul. Obviously, dreams of this kind can have great significance for self-knowledge and self-development.

We wish finally to mention prophetic dreams briefly; they are more numerous than one might think. In these cases there is a tendency to give the dream a greater importance than is justified, because the peculiar character of the dream always gives the dreaming person a feeling of having been in contact with supersensible reality. Still, various prophetic dreams that have been related belong beyond doubt to this small but important group. One of the most interesting, for various reasons, is the dream of the Bishop of Grosswardein, the teacher and friend of the Archduke Franz Ferdinand. In the early morning of the day when the Archduke was assassinated in Sarajewo, the Bishop read, in his dream, a letter written by the hand of the Archduke himself, in which he gave notice of his assassination.[58] We must imagine that in such a prophetic dream the soul is entirely free from organ-processes and desires, and also from its own inner tensions and problems, and is therefore capable of participating in events taking place in the universe or at least prepared there.

Dream and Fantasy; Memory

The relationship between dream and fantasy is well known. The same forces work in both, with the difference that in fantasy the dream-creating forces in a certain sense enter consciousness. There are countless transitional forms between dream and fantasy. In fantasy we are concerned with a release of the life-forces, which work first in shaping the organ-processes and then appear gradually in the realm of the soul.[59] This is one of the most important pedagogical issues. This complex of forces only gradually becomes free in the development of the child, and then only partly, to work in the life of the soul. The teacher's task is to develop these forces in a meaningful way in connection with the curriculum. During the first school years the child will be helped to learn in the most natural way if these forces, which are basically forces of fantasy, are guided towards artistic activities.

Someone who has not learned to use his forces of fantasy in the proper way and to make them fruitful can have the greatest disturbances later in life, because the forces of fantasy have either been pushed back or begin to grow too strongly in one way or another. Only the grace-filled artist is always able to put his forces of fantasy in the service of his life-task. For everyone else, it is of the greatest importance to learn at an early stage how to make these forces fruitful for ordinary life.

Memory, too, is related to dream and fantasy. Everyone knows from his own experience how dream-like his memories can seem. In connection with certain memory-pictures, the soul weaves in the field of memories somewhat as it does in the more elaborate dreams.

VI. The Soul in Space, Time, and Eternity

Forming Mental Images—Past; Desiring—Future;
Consciousness

Human life develops on earth within the boundaries of space and time. Philosophy has always concerned itself with the question of the essential nature of space and time. In connection with our considerations here, we will try to determine how the soul, as manifest in the human being on earth, relates to both.

As a point of departure we have chosen the words in the heading above. We have defined consciousness as a state of the soul characterized by a certain kind of knowing, a knowing that can be directed inwards, which is important especially for the soul itself. The two functions that are polar opposites, experiencing and cognizing, give rise to this kind of self-knowing. In previous chapters we attributed the emergence of consciousness to the working of the forces of life and death in the soul; we can now do this in relation to experiencing and cognizing.

The polarity of other functions comes to expression most clearly in the forces of desiring and forming mental images. In desire we recognized the source of feeling, in the forming of mental images, the terminus of judgment. Between feeling and judging the polar relationship exists, at first only as a seed. Between desiring and forming mental images, on the other hand, this polar relationship is fully developed, and here the soul experiences the greatest tension.

In this connection we will now observe these two forces more closely. Forming a mental image is always characterized by a certain accomplishment, as described above. In relation to judgment, it is in a certain sense a final state. Our cognizing relationship to the surroundings and to ourselves

121

is fixed in the mental image. When we say that in forming mental images we have to do with final states, we must concern ourselves with the past in order to reach the origin of the mental images. We can form mental images only from what has already lived in the soul. If our forming of mental images is concerned with the future, our thinking or our fantasy can indeed bring us new mental images, yet the activity out of which these mental images are formed still derives from the past.

A mental image always has the imprint of a memory. There is only a gradual difference between mental images that appear in connection with perceptions and those that arise in our memory. The difference is determined only by the time that elapses between the birth of the mental image and its reappearance in the soul. We are therefore led into the past when we examine how mental images and memories arise. If we trace this process backwards, we encounter earlier and earlier life-periods, until finally we reach the earliest years of childhood, where memory vanishes.

If one were to go still further back, one would come to the period when the soul had not yet united with the body on earth, that is, to the prenatal existence of the soul. There is no reason why this should not be possible. Usually human memory reaches back into the years of early childhood, to about the third year, that is, to the moment when the child no longer speaks about himself with his own name but begins to say "I." We have records, however, of countless childhood memories leading back to the second year, or even the first year. Adalbert Stifter even mentions memories that must be from his first weeks or months. If the soul were to develop in later life a sufficiently strong and independent force of cognition, a force that could penetrate into unconscious areas, it would be possible to retrace one's life all the way into the past, even back to the prenatal period.

It is quite different with desire. Desire expresses the urge of our "I"-hood, the kernel of our personality, to realize itself. To desire something means that we wish to unite with something outside ourself in order to provide our "I"-hood with something we believe necessary for it. Through desiring, our personality kernel tries to acquire something considered indispensable for its continued existence. The effect is that we experience in the soul a desire for intense realization of this personality kernel.

As we are led into the past through forming mental images, so we are led through desiring into the future. Every desire represents, in a certain sense, a seed, something not yet developed and that can develop fully only in the future. If we were to follow the course of desires to the end, we would come finally to the state of the soul after death, just as we could pursue the forming of mental images as far back as before birth. Desiring and forming mental images accordingly work into the soul from two different directions.

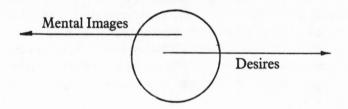

So it is that two streams of forces meet each other: one streams from the past into the future, the other from the future toward the past. Where they meet, consciousness arises.[60]

The forces working from the past carry the mental images into the soul. The stream leading to the future carries with it desire. In the soul, past and future meet in the present. Thus, the two forces of desiring and forming mental images, polarically opposite in direction, meet in the here and now. This is the secret of consciousness; it is always linked to the now, and this is why it is so difficult to grasp. When we try to describe consciousness, we have always to deal with a state of the soul that has for us the utmost reality and yet always slips away from our attempts to define it. It is the mental images or the desires and forces in the soul connected with them that arise in consciousness and drive the soul either into the past or the future. In one way or another there is always consciousness of this inner play of forces, but the clarity, breadth, and depth of this consciousness change continually.

We thus have to do with a continually changing, appearing, and vanishing "something" with which the life of the soul is most closely connected, and by which, indeed, the potential of the soul is defined. If the effect of the forces working from the past is dominant, consciousness is clearer and more sharply defined, since the mental images then have more influence. Consciousness is in that case directed mainly to the past and is not as open to the future. If, however, the desire-forces growing from out of the future enter consciousness more strongly, consciousness is less awake and less clearly defined. At the same time, it is more open to the future and the present. Ordinary waking consciousness moves continuously between these two poles and therefore changes continually in clarity as well as precision.

The Metamorphosis of Life-Forces into Consciousness-Forces; Picture-Forming

We can understand the importance of this opposition between mental images and desires more deeply if we concern ourselves with the following. Like all cognizing functions in the soul, forming mental images has a distinctly pictorial character; that is, the content of our mental images reaches us in the form of pictures. As ordinary language usage shows (in Dutch), this is true also for perceiving, thinking, and remembering, because we speak of mental pictures, percept pictures, thought pictures, and memory pictures. Although the word "picture" takes us, to begin with, into the field of visual percepts, the word in this context can have a much more comprehensive meaning. There is also a "sound-picture," created by sound or tone. In all the cognizing functions of the soul, however, we are concerned mainly with pictures that owe their origin to visual perceptions. Secondarily, we have pictures that arise from aural perceptions. Then follows—but appearing much less distinctly in consciousness—the group of pictures originating in the other senses—perceptions, such as smell, taste, etc.

Let us observe closely the pictorial character of our mental images. Through the eye and the ear, the soul lives in continual relationship with the surrounding world, and in such a way that the perceptions most important for the development of consciousness reach us through these two sense-organs. From morning till evening we are surrounded by countless pictures offered to our eyes by the world. If we add the words we speak and hear, and all the other sounds and tones around us, then by far the greater part of our consciousness is occupied. All these perceptions give rise to mental images carried by the cognizing soul as a kind of partly permanent, partly impermanent, inventory.

Here we face one of the great mysteries of the human soul. How does it come about that the universe reveals itself to the cognizing soul in such a wealth of pictures? At the beginning of this book, we indicated that the soul at birth loosens its relationship to the universe up to a certain point. Before birth the soul is permeated by the creative forces that formed and defined it. When the child is born, it is in a state of non-consciousness. Through its meeting with the world, the painful feeling emerges that a deep inner relationship, which was there previously, has been lost. This feeling changes slowly into a cognitive function, although in a primitive way, and this leads to a gradual awakening of consciousness. Through this consciousness the soul again finds in picture form the universe it had left. With a small child, this happens only in the sense that feelings of pleasure and displeasure, related to the awakening life of the desires, lead to certain perceptions and mental images. As the child grows, consciousness gradually expands and deepens; perceptions and mental images play a larger part, and finally also memory-pictures increasingly enter the life of the soul.

What is the nature of this picture-forming force, which becomes increasingly free in the soul? It is the same force that works in prenatal life and builds the body as the outer image of the developing personality. We have described previously this picture-forming force that gives body and coherent form to all living creatures. This force which, as the so-called body of formative forces, or life-body, dominates growth and propagation, is gradually set free from the life of mental images. We thus see the metamorphosis of growth-forces into consciousness-forces as the child grows older. For Steiner, this fundamental law became the foundation of his whole art of education.

Picture-Forming; Forgetting;
Organ-Processes; Education

If we examine the capacity for memory in closer connection with what was said previously, we find that we cannot assign it to a particular organ. To remember something means that we recall into consciousness something no longer present there.

To "reach beyond consciousness" means a more-or-less complete transition from soul-processes to organ-processes. This is partly so in half-conscious soul-life and entirely so in unconscious soul-life. To remember a thing, we must recover the mental images that have sunk more or less deeply into the organ-processes, and into all organ-processes, not only those in the service of the conscious life, such as the brain and other nerve systems. The organ-processes of the rhythmic system must come into consideration here, as is indicated, for example, by the expression, "to know something by heart." Everyone knows from his own experience how important the rhythmic processes are if one wishes to learn something "by heart." We try almost instinctively to group the words into a rhythmic pattern so as to bring them more easily into connection with our organism. The metabolic-limb system, that is, the man of movement, also plays a great role in this. If one learns more easily by walking and moving than by sitting still, this is caused not only by the rhythmic element in walking but by the movement itself, through which the activity of the metabolic-limb system is stimulated and made more receptive.

We must imagine the process like this: the mental images, which arise in connection with our sense-perceptions, live at first as pictures in the conscious soul. Gradually they sink through the half-conscious into the unconscious soul-life and unite there with the organ-processes. A large portion of these pictures is forgotten; that is, they fall completely into the organ processes. A smaller number is loosely connected with these processes, suspended, as it were, between organ-processes and soul-life. Nobody can retain as mental images the many thousand percept-pictures that surround one every day. Most of them sink down and are forgotten, as there is no special inner reason for the soul to unite more intensely with them. These mental images have a significance, how-ever, if not for the soul, then for the organism itself. The picture-forming force that made them unites with the pro-cesses streaming through the organism. Hence one can understand why—in addition to all the other factors—a walk in the midst of beautiful nature has an effect entirely differ-ent from that of a walk through an ugly town quarter. In the first case, we are surrounded by pictures that more or less reveal to the soul the pure being of nature and the life-forces working there. What is thereby received, even if uncon-sciously, can unite directly with the other life-processes. In the second case, the pictures do not harmonize with our own life-processes and have a disturbing effect.

In mental images we thus meet the creative or formative

127

forces already described, which permeate in their totality the human organism, and whose main characteristic is their picture-forming capacity. This capacity works plastically in the organs and organ-processes, while at the same time it is responsible for the pictorial character of mental images, memories, etc., in the soul.

We can therefore understand how it is that a small child's capacity to remember is entirely different from that of the child after the change of teeth or after puberty, because the life-forces work quite differently during different stages of development in the life of the soul. In the small child they are still entirely at work in forming the organism, in which growth and metabolism play a major role. At this stage the ability to remember is more or less fortuitous; the child may have a very good memory for certain things, while for others, none at all. The small child especially remembers anything with which he was connected in some way or another by vital interest.

After the change of teeth, when the formative forces are partially set free from their service to bodily development, another form of memory emerges. The child now can learn to memorize things in a rhythmic way. Multiplication, as well as everything else that can be patterned rhythmically, is now easier to learn. At this stage the life-forces have been partly freed in the rhythmic system. One must regard it as a serious pedagogical mistake, therefore, if children are asked before the change of teeth to memorize all manner of things. Whatever remains in the memory of its own accord at this stage is sufficient. When the child reaches school age, the rhythmic processes come into play as described above. Not until after puberty is it right to require memorizing of abstract ideas.

The Essential Nature of Desires

We encounter a great contrast when we turn from the pictorial character of thinking to the quite different character of desires. We must recognize that desires and their accompanying needs, as well as wishes and feelings, have a far greater measure of reality for us than mental images and everything related to cognition. Something that has become a picture for the soul is on that account outside the soul's inner life. We are facing it, so to speak. We can also say: the picture has an objective character for us. It is projected outside and fixed in a certain state, more or less unchangeable, ` no longer touching the inner being of the soul. In other words, the picture does not force us in a particular direction; it leaves us free.

With desires the case is entirely different. They rise into the soul from the realm of the life-forces hidden deep within us, and their real nature is intensely related to our whole personality and its continued existence. Desires continually express the demands made by our personality, whose working is for the most part hidden from us. These demands are insistent in wanting to be satisfied. They reveal with inescapable power how strenuously the personality demands its place in the world. Everyone knows the compulsive power of desires. Everyone knows, also, how much harder it is to overcome wrong desires than it is to correct false mental images, for the latter we are doing almost all the time. Only if a false mental image has a deeper meaning for us and is therefore connected in some way with our life-functions is it very difficult to uproot.

Thus mental images and desires stand in opposition to each other in the form respectively of "picture" and "being." In pictures we have a fixed and final condition of forces that have flowed into the soul from the past. In desires we have seminal forces that demand with unbridled strength their place in the life of the soul in order to reach full development in the future.

The Spatial Character of Pictures of Light and Color, Sound and Tone

We are now in a position to determine the relationship of the soul to space and time. The surrounding world, which

129

reaches us through our perceptions in the form of pictures and goes on living in our mental images and memories, is spatial in character. The whole universe, in so far as it is accessible to our perceptions, extends before us in the form of pictures. From the pictures of the stars, which limit the visible picture of the world, down to the nearest earthly phenomenon, we stand in a universe that displays itself in a vast multitude of pictures. These pictures are woven mainly of light and color but also of sounds and tones and all the other elements determining the content of our perceptions. It is mainly the realm of light and color, however, that enables us to see the spatial expanse of the universe. It is a sublime thought that the soul is able, through the sense of sight, to meet an endless number of pictures composed of light and color.

The picture-world of stars and atmospheric phenomena is thus arched above us, while we stand on the earth below with pictures of the kingdoms of nature before us.

The Time Character of "Being"; The "I"
Independent of Space and Time

When we experience inwardly the character of "being" (*zijns-karakter*) of desires, we leave the realm of space and enter the realm of time. The direction of desires towards the future is expressed in a continuing process of "becoming" and "passing away." There is no unchanging state of "being," at least not in the soul. Desires arise and seek satisfaction. When they are satisfied they seem to vanish, but they reappear after a time. Thus it goes on and on: an uninterrupted play of becoming and passing away, of living and dying, in the inner realm of the soul. For us, the essential characteristic of time is that we come to know it only by experiencing in sequence the two phases of becoming and passing away.

The kernel of the personality, or "I"-hood in the soul, connects itself with both space and time but not inseparably

130

with either. "I"-hood, as the spiritual kernel in the soul, stands above everything transient in the world of spatial and temporal relationships. This "I"-hood experiences itself in the soul, unconsciously or half-consciously, as the strongest reality that can be experienced inwardly, as "being." This same "I"-hood meets the world through the medium of the soul and gains conscious knowledge of it, but as a "picture," that is, as a reality existing outside the soul and experienced as such. In both cases, however, "I"-hood remains beyond the framework of space and time, beyond the cognitive and experiencing functions of the soul. In this context its real nature cannot be discerned, for it is rooted in eternity.

The relationship of the soul to space, time, and eternity has been given classical expression by Rudolf Steiner in the following words:

> Creature ranks with creature in the widths of Space,
> Creature follows creature in the rounds of Time.
> If you linger, O Man, in Space and Time,
> You are in realms that fade and pass away.
> But powerfully your soul will rise above them
> When you divine, or with knowledge behold, the Eternal
> Beyond the widths of Space, beyond the course of Time.[61]

Man and Woman

The soul lives on the earth in a male or female body. Certain characteristics are determined by this difference, or at least can be considered in relation to it. A warning must be given, however, against overestimating the male or the female component in the life of the soul. In the first place, the soul is "human" and therefore neither male nor female. Real "I"-hood, which we have always described as the kernel of the personality, has nothing to do with sexual differences. The human as a "spiritual being" can only be understood from the general point of view of humanity. While the highest and most profound points of view are possible here, and "I"-hood directly reveals the divine origin of the human being, this revelation is of such a tender and seedlike nature that it remains essentially hidden. This divine origin does not come directly to expression through the characteristics of the soul, the human form (*Gestalt*), and the body, but through various stages of revelation. Compared with the "I," the body is a final product in the whole process of human evolution. The human form represents a younger state; younger again is the soul, and "I"-hood is still an infant.

Thus we can understand that the highest human qualities show themselves in the soul only under the influence of "I"-hood. The sexual difference appears only in those parts of the soul connected with the body, the bodily functions, and the human form. The general human element, however, is still predominant. In a certain sense, therefore, we can distinguish masculine and feminine qualities in the soul. From what has been said previously, we can readily understand that the polarity in the soul between the cognitive and experiencing functions indicates to a great extent the difference between masculine and feminine soul qualities.

It is evident that the male soul is more prone to cognizing functions. Precise perceptions, mental images, and thoughts belong predominantly to the masculine domain; one must immediately add, however, that such statements always have a general character and that we should always look without prejudice at the whole person when making a judgment, whether the judgment concerns a man or a woman. In such matters we are always dealing with an average phenomenon, not with absolute definitions. In the male soul as much as in the female soul we find cognitive and experiencing functions in various intensities and interrelationships. Only if this is recognized can one properly draw attention to the general differences. It will then be evident that the cognitive functions play a larger part in the male soul and have a stronger influence on the whole course of a man's life on earth. His attitude and behavior are based primarily on perceiving, forming mental images, and thinking. His position in the fields of science, technology, and social enterprise indicate that this is so.

The sentient, emotional life of the female contrast with the more rational, intellectual life of the male. Her province is mainly the soul's inner experiences. Everything that comes to expression, for example, in reciprocal human relationships, in the realm of inner values, is of primary importance for the woman.

We have explored the difference between knowing and experiencing in connection with space and time. We naturally find the male a more dominant figure in the realm of spatial relationships, in house and country, and finally in the external world. The woman, by contrast, is usually more at home in the realm of the inner life, as it develops in the course of time. One could also consider, for example, the different positions held by men and women in the family. The family's external livelihood, social position, and advancement in a social sense tend more to be the responsibility of the man, while the inner life, the relationships among the family members through all periods of life, depend more upon the woman.

The difference is most apparent if we observe how men and women relate to the worlds of "picture" and "being." A man naturally feels more at home in the world of pictures. He usually has a natural ability to read and to use pictures. This is particularly evident if one watches young boys playing and sees how readily they are able to deal with quite complicated mechanisms. They have no need, for example, to know anything about mechanics or electricity in order to handle phenomena in this field in an appropriate way. They read the language of pictures spoken by the things themselves. Later, they develop these abilities in scientific, technical, and social fields. The grown man then learns how to explore the phenomena surrounding him as pictures, to analyze them, and to reconstruct them. In brief, he learns to apply the world of pictures to the service of life.

For the woman this picture-world is not so important. She seeks rather for the essential in the phenomena of life, for the "being" revealing itself in them. For her, the main point is not how something presents itself, or what it seems to be, but what it *is*. The little girl looks after her dolls with the same care that the woman later bestows on her children. In her relationships to other human beings, we can observe the same direct connection of the woman with essentials. The good or bad qualities of a person have a much more direct meaning for her. G.V.D. Leeuw articulated this difference:

> Woman is the bearer of life; she has a direct access to life, which is lacking in men; she has a closeness to life that terrifies a man and attracts him at the same time. The male is directed towards the surrounding world; he lives under the condition of the distance. But the female carries life within herself.[62]

The man, accordingly, tends to have a better and more natural relationship to the outer world and its manifold phenomena, while the woman feels united in a natural way with the inner conditions of people and things, as determined by their inner being.

For both man and woman, life on earth is a task that aims at uniting these opposites. Both strive consciously or unconsciously to be whole human beings. The man tries to reach the state of "being" through the world of "pictures"; his life will remain unsatisfied and empty if he does not succeed in finding his way—at least in some sense—to the existential nature of the human being and the world. So-called objectivity, which on the average is more akin to the male soul than to the female, becomes an empty shell if a meeting with "being" does not take place. The woman, starting from the state of "being," tries to understand the language of "pictures." Her life of feeling will be prone to errors and

134

excesses if the subjective side of her nature cannot find support in a certain objectivity given her through her meeting with the world of pictures.

The male and the female soul, therefore, develop in different directions. The man goes from the periphery to the center, from outside inwards. The woman finds her nature just in this center and strives from there out to the periphery; her way is from inside outwards. The male and the female soul, and also the masculine and feminine qualities in every human soul, are thus dependent on each other. A healthy, complete development requires that these opposites meet and overcome their one-sidedness, so that a full unfolding of human nature becomes possible. The human being is finally neither male nor female, but male-female; the term "human" (Dutch *mens*, German *Mensch*) is not an abstraction hovering somewhere between man and woman. In fact, the real nature of the human being is to be understood only through a synthesis of the polarities.

VII. The Expressive Capacity of the Soul

"Being" Forces and "Picture-Forming" Forces;
Unconscious and Conscious

Between "I" and world is the realm of the soul. We described the soul at the beginning as an inner world, where two different realities reveal themselves: on the one hand, the so-called outer world with all its phenomena; on the other, the inner world of the spirit, rising from unknown depths, which reveals itself to the soul as the "I." That these realities are essentially one was explained in a previous chapter. Here we need only mention that the so-called outer world is not less spiritual in origin than the world of which the "I" brings tidings; only the manner in which they reveal themselves is different. The world speaks to the soul in the language of pictures, while "being" rises from profound depths of the soul. From inside outwards stream the forces of "being" in the soul; as these forces move outwards, pictures are formed in the soul through contact with the world. The soul makes the world into a picture. This is characteristic of the cognizing soul: the reality of the world appears to it but only as a picture. The experiencing soul, however, is directly in "being"; that is, it lives in reality itself (see diagram).

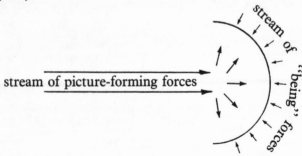

stream of picture-forming forces

If we regard the soul as a whole, we are concerned with a stream of forces of "being" in which the kernel of the personality, "I"-hood, expresses itself as reality. At the moment when this stream of forces, on its way from inside outwards, comes into its relationship to the world, it encounters a second stream of forces, by which the first is held back, even dammed up.

From this encounter, pictures arise. They replace the flowing experience of "being" with the experience of more-or-less enduring pictures and in doing so bring about waking consciousness. In so far as the soul is embraced in the stream of "being," it is *unconscious*; the soul is conscious when it is taken up into the picture-forming stream. The usual daily life of the soul alternates between unconscious and conscious, between "being" and "picture." Steiner characterized this process: "Our life consists in this—that the inner is continually becoming an outer."[64]

The whole life of the soul is interior in the sense that it embraces the whole of inner experience, but we must distinguish—in accordance with what we have just said—between the real inside, which lives in the stream of "being," and the outside, which reveals itself to the inside in the form of pictures.

The soul lives through perception, formation of mental images, memory, and thinking in a realm that has become outer in relation to the inner being of the soul itself, or, as Steiner said: "The present moment is that which is actually present within man; all past has become an exterior, so to speak." Not only is the present moment there, but also the future, though only as a seed.

The soul lives with the drives, desires, and positive feelings in the stream of "being." The nature of "being" is determined by its direct connection with the "I." The transition from the experiencing to the cognitive realm takes place in the sphere of feelings at the point where positive feelings turn into negative ones. The pictorial character comes more and more into the foreground through judgment, perception, and formation of mental images.

The Body, the Organ-Systems, Types, Form (Gestalt)

From what we have said previously, it will be clear that the soul-life is characterized by an urge to form its inner being into a picture. The whole capacity of the soul to express itself is based on this. Every such expression is finally externalized experience; it is the visible picture of an inner state of being. The further this expression has penetrated into the world, the more clearly it is recognizable as a picture. In ordinary daily life, an inner reality is most easily recognized as a picture when it takes the form of a physical imprint. A carving in wood or stone, for example, can obviously be recognized as a picture more easily than can a word-picture or thought-picture, because it is more solidly fixed in the outer world.

The human body is the picture formed directly by man as a spiritual being. It is in a certain sense the imprint of the personality, an expression of the "I." In the whole human body with all its parts (skeleton, nerves, senses, muscles, metabolic organs, etc.), we find an external expression of the personality, of the "I." The fixity characteristic of picture-forming has in this case progressed so far that the bodily image of the human being has actually become something external to the realm of the soul. It has itself become world. The organs and organ-systems are less fixed than functions and processes of the body, while the drives, which we described as life-forces, flow directly into the soul.

The human body shows us not only the fixed image of man in the general sense but also the particular characteristics of certain types of men, and indeed of each individual. Sigaud has differentiated various types of human being, distinguishing between the "cerebral" type, the "respiratory" type, and the "digestive" type.[64] Besides these, he distinguished a "muscular" type, in whom the three other types

138

are more or less in balance. Kretschmer's theory of types is generally known.[65] He also found three major groups in his differentiation of the "asthenic," "athletic," and "pyknic" types. Building on Steiner's description of threefold man, we could distinguish three types of human being in whom the nerve-sense system, the rhythmic system, or the metabolic system would more or less predominate, while a fourth type would show the three systems in balance.

With this theory of types, we approach the question of the human form (*Gestalt*). By human form we mean something that goes beyond the body. The body and the bodily processes are to be seen as bearers of human characteristics in a more general, organic sense, but in the human form the nature of man as personality, as "I," is expressed. The upright posture and the resulting ability to move the arms freely, the special form of arms, hands, and fingers, of legs and feet, the position of the head and the torso: all this defines to a large extent the picture of man as a spiritual being, as "I." "The whole human form stands like the foundation pillar of the vault, where the heavens are to be mirrored," said Goethe, when he attempted to characterize the truly human aspect of the bodily structure.

The vaulted, spherically formed skull, carried high on the vertical torso, the feet walking over the earth, and the hands freely moving in all directions are characteristics of the whole human being. Endless variety is shown in the form, the structure, the shapes and lines of individuals. Man reveals through the picture of his human form his spiritual being, and every individual shows something of this through the special configuration by which his form is characterized.

Temperament and the Human Form

Temperament is closely connected with the human form. The slim bodily stature and the big head of the melancholic, the short, stout stature of the choleric, the heavy body of the phlegmatic, with a tendency to roundness, and the harmonious slim build of the sanguine are all well known. We will not go further here into the nature of the temperaments, but will point only to their relationship to the human form on the one hand and to the personality on the other.

We can regard the temperament as an expression of the whole personality, but one that is less fixed than the body, the bodily processes, and the human form. Indeed, no part of the personality is entirely fixed. Important changes can occur even in the body in the course of time, but so slowly that it takes years for them to become noticeable. One's temperament can change under the influence of many factors. Life situations, significant events, illnesses and the like, but especially self-development and inner schooling, have the greatest influence on temperament. In a child we tend to find *one* temperament predominating. In the adult, the temperament given by nature is often in the background, having been changed under the influence of the whole soul and spiritual life. In great personalities, scholars, artists, etc., temperament will not determine the nature or quality of their works but will influence to a greater or lesser degree the form in which they appear (e.g., Nietzsche, Beethoven).

Character

We will mention only one aspect of character as an expression of personality. Modern psychology has tried for a long time to reach a correct concept of character. Here character is to be understood as a projection of the whole personality, that which is revealed by the soul in certain habits, in a certain inner formation and outer life-style.

The word "character" is used in various ways. We speak, for example, of a good, honest, or weak character. In these cases, however, we would rather speak of the manner, nature, and habit of the individual, reserving the word "character"

140

to refer to the sum of characteristics engraved in an individual's life and soul during his development, a meaning the word itself suggests. Hence we have to do here with a certain fixity, but one that occurs only during the course of life. Character in our sense emerges only as the result of change and development in a man's life. It becomes evident early in one person, later in another, strongly in some, less so in others. Older people who have always been faithful to certain inner principles, who have lived in accordance with ethical and religious standards, will generally have the most character.

Posture, Gesture, Expression, Sound, Word, Thought;
Vowels and Consonants

The body, the bodily processes, and the human form are thus the most fixed expressions of the personality. Temperament and character are more flexible, influenced more by inner factors of growth and development. Most variable of all are the expressions rising directly from the soul-life, through the interaction of the soul with the world on the one hand and with the personality kernel on the other.

Bodily expressions include posture, gesture, facial expression, and finally, every movement and action. In the realm of the soul, expressions occur through sounds and words, and in the spiritual realm through thoughts. In each of these three groups, the three main forces of the soul—thinking, feeling, and willing—are at work. They always appear together but always with different emphasis.

In posture and gesture an inner experience is always expressed, either a feeling, a will-impulse, or even a judgment. Our posture can indicate acceptance or rejection, pride or subservience, and so on. Through gestures we express endless shades and gradations in the life of the soul. The child, the primitive man, the artist, the emotional person, and the person with a spontaneous will-nature generally have a greater richness of gesture than does the modern intellectual. In the south and east of Europe, people speak a more vivid language with hands and arms than they do in the north and west. This also applies to facial expression. We need only think of children and emotional people, whose feelings are written on their faces, and compare them with the impassive faces of the average person of the twentieth century.

With individual sounds we express the spontaneous reactions of our feelings. Before arriving at the stage of words and sentences, for which a certain level of consciousness is required, we may already have expressed with a single vowel the particular feeling that has arisen within us. In the "ah"-sound lives a feeling of astonishment, amazement, and surprise. With the "o" we express a certain inner participation, whether assent or hesitation. "Au" accompanies a sensation of pain; "eh" expresses antipathy; "ei" has a judging, mocking meaning. In laughing as well as in weeping a union between facial expression and sound occurs. In relation to laughing and weeping, we have pointed already to the opposition between the sounds "ah" and "eh" (p. 53).

Some consonants are used in a similar way: "hm" indicates reassurance or acceptance; "t" ("t-t") has a calming or warning significance; "n" ("na-na") expresses doubt; "p" ("p-p"), rejection; "s" ("ssh"), admonition to be silent.

Vowels and consonants have different functions in words. The vowels express feelings that live in the soul; consonants describe the external world. We can still find in countless words how the sounds of vowels and consonants indicate the real sense and content of the word. A few examples may clarify this. The first audible expression of the soul has the "ah"-sound. One could say that the "ah"-sound appears where the soul begins to make itself audible in the outstreaming air. This is like a deepening of the stream of breath itself. In children's language this is expressed in the first words, such as Mama or Papa. When the

142

outstreaming air is to some degree withheld or compressed, the "eh"-sound emerges. Now the soul is no longer living without resistance in the outstreaming air but takes hold of it. An inner contact takes place. In this connection the difference in the Dutch language between *ja* and *nee* (yes and no) is a good example. In the "ee"-sound the stream of breath is taken hold of still more strongly but now in such a way that the soul, even the "I," lives consciously in it. In Dutch words such as *ik, licht, liefde* (I, light, love), the "ee"-sound has its special meaning. "Ah," "eh," and "ee" in a way represent the three states of consciousness: half-conscious, conscious, and self-conscious.

In the "o"-sound, the soul goes out with the flow of breath and has a tendency to embrace or at least touch something external. In the "u"-sound, this movement has come to an end; "ei" and "au" are compounds that can be understood in terms of their parts.

It may seem easy to criticize such characterizations, for it is obviously possible to cite words where these relationships are not evident, but that is not the point. One must try to reach an *inner experience* of what the sounds themselves express. Certain words seem typical in this respect, others do not. A detailed study of the origin of words is required, through which one becomes aware of the changes over the centuries regarding how words are written and their meaning. What we have suggested here is merely an indication of possibilities. For further information, refer to the relevant literature.[66]

The difference between the inner nature of vowels and of consonants coincides with the polarity between the experiencing and the cognizing soul. The vowels express our spontaneous emotional movements and are thus closely connected with the inner being of the soul. The consonants have more to do with describing, cognizing, and characterizing relationships to things and hence have a stronger pictorial character. One could compare, for example, the "w"

in waves and wind; the "r" in roll, rattle, and rustling; and
the "d" in the Dutch *de, die, dat,* and *daar.*

The Word

A word as a whole cannot, however, be understood from
its constituent sounds only. It is more than the sum of its
vowels and consonants. It is, in fact, a sound-picture in
which we express our encounter with a reality in the world
or within ourselves. One can also regard a word as a sense-
image, born from sounds that reflect the inwardly experienced and outwardly observed reality of things and phenomena. The most intimate meeting that takes place between
the human being and the world or among people is reinforced
by the word. This is the reason that in the old religions and
philosophies the word has been held sacred. Things are
born out of the "logos," out of the creative Word, which
was "in the beginning" and through which everything has
come into being. As St. John said when he spoke about the
Word: "All things were made by Him; and without Him
was not anything made that was made." The same thought
is also expressed in different ways in the ancient mysteries
of India, Persia, and Egypt. Only when the creative word
sounds out of the human being in such a way that he has
become a creator in the world of the spirit, only then has he
become truly "human." Before that he was God's creation,
entirely led and determined by divine forces. He has not yet
become a fully independent being, fighting between the
forces of good and evil out of his own drive for development
and freedom.

The birth of the personality is connected with the power
to speak the word or to give things their names:

> . . . And out of the ground the Lord God formed
> every beast of the field, and every fowl of the air;
> and brought them unto Adam to see what he would

144

call them: and whatsoever Adam called every living creature, that was the name thereof. (Genesis 2:14)

The word is thus the highest sense-picture that arises in man as a divine being, in order to express his relationship to the universe. In ancient times the utterance of this relationship was rightly regarded as sacred, for it brought about a meeting of spirit with spirit, the human spirit with the divine spirit of the world. Such a relationship is at the same time creative, since it is not passively accepted but must grow out of man again and again as a free deed.

Through the word, man places himself as a being of divine-spiritual nature in the universe. His origin and his destination are revealed through his power to speak the word, by which he becomes a creator in his own world, just as the Divine Almighty is the Creator in the universe.

In modern times, the sacred word of the ancients is all but forgotten. Ever since the eleventh century, following the development of intellectual consciousness, with its attention focused on external phenomena, the possibility of penetrating into the deeper essence of sounds and words has more or less faded. By degrees the word has been made to serve predominantly the labeling and description of things. It has in large measure lost its spiritual content and has become a sign or formula which the soul, oriented towards the intellect and the senses, manipulates. Only poets and philosophers continue to seek the word's deeper meaning. They have painfully experienced how the word has become a corpse, bereft of soul and spirit. "For us only the now was left without a soul," said Schiller in his poem, "The Gods of Greece."

In our own time, especially, a true relationship to the word seems lost. Any arbitrary composition of letters is accepted as a so-called word in daily life. In this respect, our age has become completely nominalistic. A name (*nomen*) is a collective term for many single things. "The word," said Boethius, "is a movement of air, produced by the tongue."[67]

While one may not share this radical view, there is scarcely an alternative, a deeper perspective, offered in our culture. Yet the golden thread, which in the quest for the deeper meaning of the word leads back into antiquity, is not entirely broken. Plato, the Evangelists, the great poets of German Idealism (Herder, Goethe, Novalis), to mention only a few examples, bears witness to the possibility of letting the deeper spiritual sense of a word resound. In addition to the ordinary use of a word, we see many artists, scientists, and philosophers striving to bring the lost word of creation to rebirth in human speech.

Word, Concept, Idea

As a word is more than its component sounds, so is a thought more than the words from which it is formed. With this view, we approach in a certain sense the standpoint of the medieval Realists, for whom a thought was closer to the truth—that is, to the spiritual reality—the more universal it was. According to the Realists, the general is closer to "being" than the particular. Our way of expressing it is that a thought or idea begins with the stamp of "being" and then becomes more and more a picture as it is related to the outer things. The highest and profoundest thoughts are the most difficult to express in words, because the pictorial character of words is not entirely able to reach the "being" that lives in such thoughts.

The word is born with the sounds yet at the same time *in* the sounds, just as the soul comes to earth with and in the body. Words are thus necessary in order for concepts and ideas to reveal themselves with and in the words as spiritual expressions of the soul. With the word "concept" (*begrip*), we wish to indicate the activity of soul that can be correctly described as an inner grasping of a spiritual content. Only

146

when we have grasped or understood something inwardly does it become our own. The word "idea" (*denkbeeld*) connotes that this spiritual content has become a picture (*beeld*) and indeed a purely spiritual picture.

In this we have reached the highest expressive possibilities of the soul and of the spirit working in it. In word, concept, and idea, man reveals his highest characteristic as an ensouled divine-spiritual personality. Here we are in an area free from any outer fixity. Words and thoughts are born in the soul and are offered to the world when they are uttered. They are carried on a continuous stream of forces without becoming hardened. Man speaks and thinks in a continuously living, moving, and variable realm, and there he meets his fellow men, living and communicating with them in the purely human sphere.

Inner Relationship of Posture, Speech, and Thought;
Creative and Associative Thinking

There is a deep inner relationship among the upright posture, speech, and thought. We must imagine the possibilities given to the human being through not being bound to the horizontal surface of the earth like an animal but being able to stand upright, oriented vertically towards heaven. The paw has become a foot whose sole touches the earth in walking. The whole process of human walking is composed of three parts: lifting the foot from the earth, carrying forward movement; and a touching in placing the foot down. Here is expressed a free relationship between body and earth that can also be experienced in the soul while walking. The upper limbs are released from the task of helping the body to move in space, a task for which they are no longer needed. Arms and hands are slimmer in form and can move in almost any direction. The hands have become organs for both touching and expressing. They accompany words with gestures; they enable man to express himself in

147

writing as well as to practice the most difficult and delicate of handicrafts.

The lungs have been placed above the diaphragm through the upright position, and the chest is no longer a horizontal annex to the stomach, as it is in the animal. The forces of desire, connected with the animalistic functions, have in animals a direct continuation in the breathing process. These organs have been given a place in the human being that helps free him from drives and desires. This has made speaking possible, whereas the animal is able to make only sounds deriving directly from its drives and desires.

Finally, the position of the head as the crown of the human frame forms the basis for those modes of expression in which is revealed man's spiritual origin. The receding mouth has replaced the jaws or snout of the animal. Animalistic forces are withheld there so that human capacities may be born. The receding mouth corresponds with the rising forehead and the entire vaulted skull. The head's position on the body is such that the front and back of the head are approximately equidistant from the vertebrae; in relation to the whole frame, the head is thus in a state of balance. This makes it possible for thoughts to be mirrored in the head.

Without the upright posture, the human being would not be able to speak. "The divine gift of speech" (Herder) could be lodged only in a body which through its unique structure allows man to be the carrier of the word. The uniqueness of our form is also revealed in the position of our speech-organs. They are part of our rhythmic system, since they are directly connected with the lungs, yet they retain an independent position.

The lungs and the larynx, the mouth and the lips form a single, related organ-area, which includes even the arms and the hands as organs of expression that accompany speech. This organ-area is connected on one side with the blood and metabolism and on the other side with the senses, brain, and nerves. It therefore lies midway between the two polar organ-systems. This has great significance. Words spoken by the human being could not arise except from the middle area. Regarding the relationships of sounds, of vowels and consonants, we find in every word a certain balance. In the animal kingdom, only sounds occur. The hee-haw of the donkey, the moo of the cow, even the songs of the birds, including the nightingale, consist exclusively of sounds. A word is formed through vowels and consonants creating a balanced, harmonious whole. In that "whole" lies the secret of the word, making it a sense-picture for inner or outer reality.

The word is born in a stream of soul-forces that unite with the outstreaming air. The vowels rise from the deeper realm, from out of the experiencing soul, and therefore from feeling and desiring. The consonants are related, as mentioned above, to the cognizing soul, to the forming of judgments and mental images. For the vowels to emerge, it is sufficient for the stream of speech, directed from inside outwards, to be more or less compressed or redirected. The consonants are formed when the formative forces of the cognizing soul work on the stream of speech from outside. This "working" can be regarded as a kind of modeling or sculpture.

The whole soul participates as each word arises, and with the soul the body also participates. In the imagery of the ancient teachings about the four elements, we could say that the four elementary forces at work in the solid, the liquid, the gaseous, and the warmth all take part in the process of speaking. A stream of warmth flows out with the exhaled air, a degree of humidity of the speech-organs is necessary, and the sounds—especially the consonants—are audible only through the air's contact with the solid surroundings of these organs.

In connection with our previous considerations, we can point here to the interaction between the building, nourishing forces of the metabolic system, the life-forces already described, and the disintegrative, consciousness-forming forces of the nerve-sense system, with its picture-forming capacity. These forces stream together in the rhythmic system and are balanced and harmonized there.

Like the word, thought also depends directly on man's upright posture. Steiner repeatedly drew attention to the fact, so important in this connection, that the human brain loses most of its weight through the buoyancy it gains from the liquid surrounding it. If its weight is 1375g and its volume 1330ccm, then the brain, with its specific weight of 1035g, presses down with only a little weight on its base. This means that the brain is an organ located in a system of predominantly upward-working forces, forces that strive away from the earth and are therefore opposite to the force of gravity. These counter-gravitational forces are mostly withdrawn from those parts of the organism where earthly influences predominate; hence they can provide a basis for the cognitive soul-functions, especially for forming mental images.

Goethe rightly distinguished two modes of thinking, assigning one to reason (*Vernunft*), the other to intellect (*Verstand*). "Reason," he said, "is concerned with whatever is in the process of becoming; the intellect is concerned with what has already become. Reason does not ask, from where? The intellect does not ask, for what? Reason likes development; the intellect would like to keep everything fixed in order to make use of it."[68]

The intellect is equipped to understand only whatever has finished developing. This applies to things and phenomena on earth that show in their formation that they have reached a certain finality. The senses and the intellect can deal with them. The process of becoming, of being in the course of development, cannot be directly perceived by the senses. A thinking man, however, is able, through ideas or thought-pictures, to grasp inwardly the process of development and so understand it. Examples of such ideas are

150

Goethe's idea of the archetypal plant and his idea of the metamorphosis of plants. Goethe was in agreement with the medieval Realists, for whom concepts, thoughts, and ideas were spiritual realities, not merely names that men added to the phenomena from outside to distinguish or to connect them. For Goethe, the creative forces working in nature are hidden only in so far as man cannot perceive them with his senses. He must develop a higher, more ideal cognitive capacity to be able to enter their world.

"Nature hides God . . . but not from everyone," Goethe added;[69] that is, the divine secrets are revealed only to the thinking man, in whom are born the ideas that encompass the processes of becoming in nature herself.

Steiner characterized this thinking capacity of the human being in the following way: "Thinking is an organ of perception just as are the eye and the ear. Thought is related to our minds just as light is to the eye and tone to the ear."[70]

In our time, the experience of the reality of thoughts has been lost, or at least weakened, just as much as that of the reality of the word. The difference between associative thought and creative thinking is, of course, known, but people generally hesitate to recognize the radical difference between the two. Scheler precisely characterized this difference with his remark that "there is only a graduated difference between a clever chimpanzee and Edison."[71] Edison is, of course, considered only as a technician in this remark. The "graduated difference" is obviously very large, but the capacities of both are in the field of intellectual combination. The thinking capacities transcending this intellectual level are indicated by Scheler with the general term "spirit."

Steiner pointed repeatedly to the difference between living and dead thinking. He thus called mental images, as they appear in ordinary consciousness, "thought-corpses," or he spoke of "passive" as opposed to "active" thinking. Living, active thoughts are possible only in the human being. They belong, together with the upright posture and speech, to the human characteristics revealing that man is in reality a spiritual being who can walk, speak, and think in a balance of body, soul, and spirit—and thereby live on the earth as the "marvelous stranger, with the expressive eyes, the floating step, and the tenderly closed lips, rich in sounds," that Novalis described.[72]

VIII. The Soul and the Threefold Nature of Man

The Three-Times-Threefold Human Being

At the beginning of our considerations we described the soul in its relationship to the outer world of the body and the inner world of the spirit. The polar tendencies of the forces working in the soul were comprehensible in terms of those relationships. In the middle, between the two poles, and indeed permeated by them, lies the true realm of the soul. Working from out of this middle region are the forces that unite and harmonize the two poles, creating a unity out of trinity. We thus come to a picture of the threefold nature of the soul, which is expressed in the body in the three systems of organs, already described, with which the whole life of the soul is closely related. Its ultimate origin, however, is in the spirit, the kernel of the personality, the "I," which works in the soul through three forces: thinking, feeling, and willing.

The threefold nature of the soul, therefore, can be understood only in relation to the threefold nature in which the whole being of "man" appears before us. In the body we have three organ-systems: the nerve-sense system, the rhythmic system, and the metabolic-limb system; in the soul, three groups of functions: forming mental images, judging, and feeling-desiring; and, in the spirit, three main forces: thinking, feeling, and willing.

As the threefoldness in the soul-life can be traced to an essential unity, so it is with the three-times-threefold man. This train of thought does not lead to a dualism of body and soul, nor to their equation on the ground of the continuous relationships between them. On the contrary, we understand the whole structure of the human being in body, soul, and spirit only if we find the trinity shown in the functions of the soul, and even precisely trace the soul's development into the body on one side and into the realm of spirit on the other.

The "I"; The Picture-Forming Forces; Thinking

The realm of the spirit, from which the "I" allows its forces to radiate into body and soul, remains hidden from ordinary methods of cognition. Neither with sense-perception nor with the intellect do we enter the world of the spirit. We learn to understand the "I" as such only indirectly, through the upright position and the characteristic human form, through the unity that underlies all organ-processes and through the reciprocal interplay of the soul-processes. The "I" also manifests itself in will-impulses, feelings, and thoughts. Finally it appears in consciousness as the mental image of the "I," which accompanies all other mental images.

Yet the "I" remains hidden; it is the eternal entelechy, the divine spark that brings about the appearance of the whole human being as an autonomous unity but that never unveils itself. We can nevertheless gain access to the world in which the "I" is living, the world of the spirit. This we can do by developing our cognitive faculties further and, with their aid, finding our way to the essential nature of the three archetypal forces, thinking, feeling, and willing. These three forces are *the three knowable aspects of the "I."* The encounter with their primal spiritual nature is on the frontier of our perceptive capacity. It can take place in the following way. We have already distinguished the pictorial character (*beeld-karakter*) of the cognitive functions from the character of "being" (*zijns-karakter*) belonging to the experiencing part of the soul. This pictorial character finds its highest expression in the ability of the soul to express itself in ideas (*denkbeelden*). We further discussed the pictorial character of our mental images, memories, and words; and

154

finally we pointed to the whole appearance of man, whose body and form reveal a picture of the "I."

This picture-forming force is certainly the same in all these forms and activities. If we go still further and search through the whole outer human world, we always find these same picture-forming forces in the endless variety of forms that living nature produces, as well as in so-called inanimate nature. In ordinary consciousness the whole world appears to us in the form of pictures, the inanimate and the animate, including man. The forces that work in these pictures and cause them to appear can best be investigated where this process of picture-forming takes place in the soul itself, particularly in the conscious soul, where ideas and living thoughts arise. Something takes place there that would not happen without our participation, and at the same time we can follow the whole process step by step. Steiner said: "When a man thinks, he himself can observe the activity which he pursues in thinking," concluding, "This then is indispensable: in thinking we have grasped the one part of the world-process that requires us to be present if anything is to happen."[73]

The force active in human thinking is of the same kind as the force that creates the manifold forms in nature. To our sense-perception, nature appears in pictures, in percepts. The picture-forming force itself, however, works in our soul as a thinking-force (denk-kracht), as a force that makes possible the forming of ideas. In the further development of consciousness, the point is not only to make these picture-forming forces conscious in the soul but also to strengthen them. It lies beyond the limits of this book, however, and also outside the field of psychology, to describe the method of this developmental process or its foundation in epistemology. We can only refer briefly to the relevant literature.[74]

The first stage in such a development that goes beyond

ordinary consciousness leads to so-called imaginative consciousness. Imaginative consciousness is related to ordinary waking consciousness as waking consciousness is related to dreaming. In light of what we have said about the significance of picture-forming forces in dreams, we can say that the forces working in the half-conscious, which create dream-pictures, come into the full light of consciousness in forming imaginations. Imaginations, therefore, are not fantasies or fancies but spiritual pictures, observed in full consciousness.

The picture-forming forces reveal themselves in imaginative consciousness. They are the basis of thinking, of the forming of mental images and memories. The creative soul lives in these forces when ideas arise, ideas in Goethe's sense. Forming mental images is essentially the same process, but with the difference that the living thought-forces crystallize in the mental images, so that only a fixed and therefore dead imprint of them remains in the soul (compare p. 71).

While the world of the cognizing soul is thus characterized by pictures, the world of the living soul is characterized by "being." Feelings and desires have the character of "being," but this is entirely true only of desires. Feelings, with their polar structure of pleasure and displeasure, sympathy and antipathy, etc., belong to that part of the soul lying midway between knowing and experiencing, which is why we include desiring as an experience of the soul.

In the world of feelings we always find a peculiarly ambivalent relationship. Feelings belong essentially to the realm of "being," but they always tend to pass over into the realm of pictures. We described this peculiarity in discussing the origin of judgments in connection with negative feelings (compare pp. 36–37). To get to know the feelings that work as the second spiritual archetypal force in all phenomena of the feeling-life, a further development of the cognitive capacities is required. In addition to imaginative consciousness, inspirational consciousness must develop, based on a

156

carefully practiced control and harmonization of the feelings of sympathy and antipathy. In ordinary soul-life, consciousness diminishes if the feelings become stronger. One must therefore achieve through careful training a state of active equanimity, that is, a strong conscious life in the feeling realm of the soul. Feelings of sympathy and antipathy then lead to a deepening of the consciousness, because they bring the soul into contact with those qualities of things and appearances that can reveal themselves to the soul only through feelings. Instead of clouding the consciousness, feelings now become organs through which a higher form of perception is possible. In imaginative consciousness the soul is faced with living spiritual pictures, whereas in inspirational consciousness is revealed the world of "being," of spiritual reality, but in such a way that these pictures partly hide their reality. Inspirations are pictures through which radiates spiritual presence. The dual nature of feelings in their relation to "being" and "picture" also appears here.

The soul can enter the world of "being" entirely if the path of development is continued in such a way that those forces forming the basis of the life of desires and drives are consciously controlled and purified. This third stage of development, called "intuitive consciousness," was characterized by Steiner with the expression, "Love must here become the power of knowledge." Through intuitive consciousness, one comes to know the third spiritual archetypal force that works in the soul: the will.

Through the development of imagination, inspiration, and intuition, man successively enters into the world of living spiritual pictures, where *thinking* has its origin; the world where pictures are permeated by spiritual reality and wherein lies the origin of *feeling*; and finally the world where the spiritual reality itself appears and wherein lies the origin of *willing*.

The following diagram may clarify the relationship of the soul to body and spirit.

Body	Soul	Spirit
Nerve-Sense System Images, Judging	Forming Mental Images (Imagination)	Pure Thinking
Rhythmic System (Inspiration)	Feeling	Pure Feeling
Metabolic-Limb System	Desiring	Pure Willing (Intuition)

Imagination; Inspiration; Intuition

Through this threefoldness, the deeper relationships among body, soul, and spirit become evident. The picture-forming forces, which are the foundation of thinking in the spirit, work in the soul as forces for forming mental images and memory, and also in all expressions that have a pictorial character. In the body they finally find expression in the formative forces that make the body visible to the eye. This applies in the first place to the system of organs we have described as the nerve-sense system. The senses, the brain, the spinal fluid with the nerves and ganglia, and also the whole sympathetic nerve system, show this pictorial character to a high degree. They are all more or less direct imprints of the cognitive functions characteristic of the soul.

In the eye, light created an organ for itself, by which the phenomena of light could become perceptible. In the same way, the spiritual force of thinking formed the brain in order to have an organ where these thinking forces could appear as mental images in the conscious soul-life. The further organs of the central and sympathetic nerve systems are also to be regarded in connection with these thinking forces, which are active in the half-conscious or unconscious areas as formative forces in the organs.

The forces in the spirit that are the basis of feeling are expressed in all emotional phenomena of the experiencing soul. Their ambivalent nature in relation to "picture" and "being" appears in the body in the particular functions of the rhythmic system. The breathing process of the lungs, the blood circulation with the heartbeat, and all the other rhythmic processes show a continually alternating expansion and contraction, or systole and diastole. Seen from the spirit, feeling brings about the inner relationship and harmonization of thinking and willing, by which these two, together with feeling, become the unity we have called the "I." In the soul, feeling forces bring about the balance

Widening of Consciousness
at the same time:
Development of a Spiritual Universal Consciousness

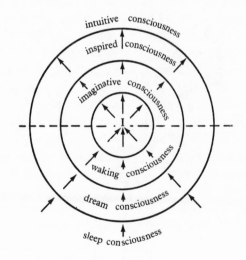

Narrowing of Consciousness
at the same time:
Concentration towards "I"-Consciousness

159

between forming mental images and desiring. We must always deal with all three together, but in an ever-changing relationship. In the body, finally, it is again the rhythmic processes that unite the nerve-sense system and the In the body, finally, it is again the rhythmic processes that unite the nerve-sense system and the metabolic-limb system.

Willing as a spiritual archetypal force has the most hidden life in the soul; it rises as a nearly unconscious force from the life-impulses into the desires. In the body it works as the actual life-force in all functions of the metabolic-limb system, hence in nutrition, growth, and propagation. Thus the whole human appearance in body, soul, and spirit is a revelation of the spiritual man who, as the "I" in its three aspects of thinking, feeling, and willing, permeates and rules the soul and gives to the body life and form in a threefold manner.

IX. The Development of the Soul Through the Forces of Wisdom and Love

Concerning Love

The worlds between which the soul lives, the outer and the inner worlds, are both of spiritual origin. In each the soul meets the spirit but in different ways. In the outer world the manifold forms and phenomena of nature appear: the crust of the earth with its plains, mountains, and valleys, the oceans and rivers, the air with the mists and clouds, and finally the heavenly vault where we can see the stars and planets by night. In the midst of this outer world are the stones, the metals, and the crystals, the thousandfold forms of plants and trees, the nearly endless variety of animals, and, at last: the human being.

All this conjures up for the soul a world of pictures, which in its smallest part reflects an immeasurable wisdom, a wisdom before which man bows again and again in deep reverence, and before which he continuously feels the greatest admiration rising within himself. The construction of a crystal, even a grain of sand, reveals to us the cosmic laws we again find in the structure of the universe. The life-functions of a one-cell organism are ordered according to the same principles as those of the higher animals. The large is mirrored in the small; the small speaks the same spiritual language as the large. This has come about in accordance with a plan of creation whose wisdom we encounter in all phenomena.

When the soul gradually awakens on earth, it encounters the pictures in which the world reveals itself, and a desire arises to understand the language of these pictures; in other words, the cognizing soul has an inborn striving for wisdom.

161

The soul relates in an entirely different way to the inner world. At first this inner world makes itself known to the soul in only a dim, undefined way. The life-impulses and the desires connected with them are linked with changing feelings. The soul is led by them with great certainty but unconsciously. What is experienced with convincing certainty is the necessity of the desires and feelings for the existence, for the very being of soul and body. One experiences their character of "being" without understanding their true nature.

A true inner awakening is possible here, too, if one discovers that there is one force working in both desires and feelings that can lead them to a certain condition—a condition that encompasses feeling and willing and can come to expression in love. Love can express itself in manifold ways, e.g., love for nature, for compatriots, for one of the opposite sex, and finally also for humanity as such and for the high ideals that live in humanity (cf. pp. 54–55).

This love is the actual force that forms the soul from within. We have already mentioned Steiner's words, "The basic substance of the life of the soul on earth is love," and "all soul-phenomena are transformations, modifications, of love." To describe love in psychological terms is difficult. It is certain that both feeling and willing—in the highest forms in which they appear—live in love. In order to clarify the special nature of love, Steiner compared it to a glass of water that becomes more full the more water one pours out of it, a comparison which in its utter simplicity penetrates to the depth of this mystery. We know how every satisfaction of desires gives rise to an inner feeling of emptiness, while every satiation of feelings has a crippling effect on the will.

In love we have to do with a merging of two archetypal forces: feeling and willing; the soul unfolds its strongest activity in the realm of the spirit, where the "I" works into the soul. This is why love has the characteristic of inexhaustibility. Just as the creative force of nature is inexhaustible, so also is the force of love, once it has awakened in the human soul.

In order to attain this love, one must fight a great inner battle for development. The "I," as the spiritual and moral kernel of the personality, reveals in the course of this battle the two main characteristics of its nature: that it is not only inexhaustible but also merciless. Every condition in the soul not in harmony with the highest ideals is disturbed and interrupted again and again. No inner experience gives permanent rest, no desire a lasting satisfaction. A yawning void or a dull passivity emerge again and again, but new possibilities always arise. It is the force of the "I" that here brings about continous transformations, an ever-changing metamorphosis. The number of opportunities seems endless and is linked neither to time nor age. However old a man may be, as long as he continues to live and experience, as long as he desires, it is possible for love to blossom in his soul. The soul is thus led with unrelenting strength to true love and also through an endless variety of new opportunities.

Goethe wrote of this in a poem, "Blissful Longing," which opens with the words:

> Tell nobody but the wise,
> For the crowd will be quick to mock;
> I will praise the living
> Which longs for death by fire.

The Persian poet, Hafis, whom Goethe reformulated here, ended with the verses:

> Until you no longer burn like a butterfly from desire,
> You can never find salvation from the grief of love.

Goethe also used the image of the butterfly who seeks death in the flames:

> And finally, greedy of light,
> Are you butterfly-burnt.

But Goethe's version ends with the eternal words:

> Until you have learned to say
> Die and become!
> You are but a shadowy guest
> On this dark earth.

This "die and become" is the path for the soul, which rises out of the bondage of desires and feelings to the inner freedom revealing itself through the power of love. "A shadowy guest" is the man in whom this power has not yet awakened, "shadowy" in the sense Goethe gave the word: only somewhat transparent for the light that speaks to the soul out of the wisdom-filled world-order. The wisdom of which we can partake through a consciousness illuminated by the spirit works in the soul and forms the basis for the metamorphosis of desires and feelings into love.

Thus we come to know love as the most essential principle working in the soul, a truly creative and transforming force. It is the highest revelation of the "I." As long as love does not live in the soul, the realm of "being," in which spiritual man has his origin, has not yet been attained. Desires and feelings do indeed have the character of "being," but "being" remains hidden. It unveils itself entirely in love alone. The greatest human spirits have known and described this last and highest principle by which man gives expression to this divine kinship. "The greatest of them is love," wrote Paul in his first letter to the Corinthians, in which he spoke of faith, hope, and love.

In Goethe's fairy tale, the young man is led by the "old man with the lamp" to the statues of the three kings, who represent the forces "which have rule on earth: Wisdom, Appearance, and Strength." Equipped with their powers the young man says: "Glorious and secure is the kingdom of our fathers, but thou hast forgotten the fourth power, which rules the world, earlier, more universally, more certainly, the power of Love." The man with the lamp, however,

164

replies: "Love does not rule, but it educates, and that is more."[75]

Amidst the wisdom-filled revelation of the universe this metamorphosis of soul-forces goes through a continuous development, a perpetual becoming of the true nature of man. Universe and "I" are both given; they both establish inescapable norms for the soul. On earth we find the outer world, with all things, phenomena, and beings as expressions of divine creation. Through wisdom, to which the soul can ascend, we learn to understand their language of pictures. Within us, however, we also find the standards by which our divine nature expresses itself in the hidden depths of the soul. We have spoken already of truth, beauty, and goodness as the three principles to which the inner being of the soul must relate itself (compare pp. 9–10).

Man stands unfinished between the two given worlds, a being who still must achieve his real nature; he still must *become* man. "Human existence," says V.D. Leeuw, "is by no means accomplished. The animal is, God is. Man is merely given the opportunity. He is not even man; he is on the way to becoming man. His birth as Man is not finished." Or, as he says later: "Man is always on the way."[76]

This process of becoming human takes place according to the law of metamorphosis. The Mystery of Golgotha revealed for all time the eternal riddle of human development. The way of Christ leads through life and death to resurrection. A "dying and becoming" in the highest sense has thereby been fulfilled *in* and *for* humanity. "The light of the world" conquered death through the power of sacrificial love. The "I" revealed its divine and at the same time human nature as the pattern for all men, wherein they could find the *meaning* and *destination* of human life.

In this mystery, moreover, the great significance that suffering has for development was made clear. All human suffering is insignificant in comparison to the pains and violations that Christ had to endure, yet all suffering finally has the same meaning, the same task, namely, the internalization, the cleansing, the spiritualization of the human soul, so that it may become an organ for the "I," when the "I" will have found its true destination in fulfilling the words of Paul: "Not I, but Christ in me."

Here we enter the area where psychology and a philosophy of life overlap. They cannot be entirely separated. Every science is in the end a part of our views on the relationship between man and world. The cognizing soul investigates these relationships, but the living and developing soul is itself involved, and not as an interested spectator but as a growing collaborator in the great becoming of man and mankind. Any psychology wishing to be truly fruitful must respect this fact.

Notes

1. Felix Krueger, *Über Entwicklungspsychologie*, 1915.
2. *Ibid.*
3. Rudolf Steiner, *The Philosophy of Freedom* (Spring Valley, NY: Anthroposophic Press, 1964), pp. 72–3.
4. *Ibid.*
5. Rudolf Steiner, *Einfurhrung zu Goethe's Naturwissenschaftlichen Schrifter* (Stuttgart, 1883–87).
6. By Johann Joachim Becher (1635–1682).
7. Oswald Külpe, *Vorlesungen über Psychologie* (Leipzig, 1922).
8. Rudolf Steiner, *Von Seelenrätseln* (Riddles of the Soul) (Dornach: Rudolf Steiner Nachlassverwaltung, 1961), GA21. Unfortunately, the obituary essay for Brentano was omitted from the English edition published under the title *The Case for Anthroposophy* (London: Rudolf Steiner Press, 1970).
9. *Ibid.*
10. Aristotle, *de Anima* (On the Soul).
11. Franz Brentano, *Vom Ursprung sittlicher Erkenntnis*, 1899. *Psychologie vom empirischen Standpunkte*, 1874.
12. Rudolf Steiner, *Psychosophie*, four lectures, 1910.
13. Novalis, *Psychologische Fragmente*, number 462.
14. Rudolf Steiner and Ita Wegman, *Fundamentals of Therapy: An Extension of the Art of Healing Through Spiritual Knowledge* (London: Rudolf Steiner Press, 1967), GA27.
15. *Ibid.*
16. Steiner, *Philosophy of Freedom.*
17. Max Scheler, *Man's Place in Nature* (New York: Noonday Press, 1976), pp. 35–9.
18. J. Lindworsky, *Das Seelenleben des Menschen*, 1934.
19. G. Mannourry, *De toepassing van den wiskundigen denkvorm op de autopsychologie*, 1939.

20. Johann Gottlieb Herder, *Ideen zur Philosophie der Geschichte der Menschheit.*
21. Franz Brentano, *Psychologie vom Empirischen Standpunkt*, 1874.
22. Steiner, *The Wisdom of Man, The Wisdom of the Soul, and the Wisdom of the Spirit* (Spring Valley, NY: Anthroposophic Press, reprint 1971), GA115.
23. Johann Wolfgang von Goethe, *Sprüche in Prosa.*
24. Steiner, *Wisdom of Man*, p. 70.
25. Steiner, *Philosophy of Freedom.*
26. An interesting and in some ways beautiful description of the manifest forms of love is to be found in Max Scheler's *The Nature of the Sympathy* (Connecticut: Archer Books, 1970).
27. Max Scheler, *Der Formalismus in der Ethik und die materiale Wertethik*, 1921.
28. Steiner, *Wisdom of Man.*
29. *Ibid.*
30. Scheler, *Man's Place in Nature*, pp. 8-9.
31. Theodore Ziehen, *Physiologische Psychologie.* Ziehen is perhaps the most characteristic of this period.
32. Franz Brentano, *Von der Klassifikation der psychischen Phaenomene*, 1911.
33. Otto Klemm, *Geschichte der Psychologie*, 1911.
34. Brentano, *Von der Klassifikation.*
35. Schiller, *Letters on the Aesthetic Education of Man*, Letters 12-15. Compare also: B. Lievegoed, *Maat, Rythme, Melodie*, 1939, where Schiller's importance for modern psychology is characterized.
36. *Ibid.*
37. *Ibid.*
38. G.v.d. Leeuw, *Der Mensch und die Religion*, 1941.
39. Steiner, *Wisdom of Man*, p. 76.
40. Rudolf Steiner, *Der pädagogische Wert der Menschenerkenntnis und der Kulturwert der Pädagogik*, 1929.

41. Steiner, *Wisdom of Man*, pp. 86-7.
42. Novalis, *Psychologische Fragmente*.
43. Johannes Peter von Muller, *Zur vergleichenden Physiologie des Gesichtsinnes*, 1826.
44. Steiner, *The Case for Anthroposophy*.
45. *Ibid.*
46. Johann Wolfgang von Goethe, *The Metamorphosis of Plants* (Rhode Island: Bio-Dynamic Literature, 1978).
47. Refer to Rudolf Steiner's researches, and those of William Stern and Karl Buhler.
48. Scheler, *Man's Place in Nature*, pp. 51-2.
49. Rudolf Steiner, *Wahrspruchworte*, 1925.
50. Carl Gustav Carus, *Organon*, 1856.
51. Rudolf Steiner, *Was kann die Heilkunst durch eine geisteswissenschaftliche Betrachtung gewinnen?*, three lectures, 1924.
52. Karl Fortlage, *Acht psychologische Vortrage.*, 1869.
53. Goethe, *Metamorphosis*.
54. Steiner, *The Case for Anthroposophy*, pp. 69-84.
55. *Ibid.*, p. 71.
56. *Ibid.*, p. 72.
57. *Ibid.*, p. 78.
58. Mentioned by N. Glas in the journal *Natura* (February, 1927).
59. Rudolf Steiner, *Die Erziehung des Kindes vom Gesichtspunkte der Geisteswissenschaft*, 1907.
60. Rudolf Steiner, *Allgemeine Menschenkunde als Grundlage der Pädagogik*, 1932.
61. Steiner, *Wahrspruchworte*, 1925.
62. Leeuw, *Der Mensch und die Religion*.
63. Rudolf Steiner, *The World of the Senses and the World of the Spirit* (Canada, Steiner Book Centre, reprinted 1979), p. 48.
64. Claude Sigaud, *La Forme Humaine*, 1914.
65. Ernst Kretschmer, *Korperbau und Charakter*, 1922.

66. See Beckhe, *Etymologie und Lautbedeutung* and *Der physische und der geistige Ursprung der Sprache*. Rudolf Steiner, *Eurythmy as Visible Speech*.
67. Boethius.
68. Goethe, *Spruche in Prosa*.
69. *Ibid.*
70. Rudolf Steiner, *A Theory of Knowledge Implicit in Goethe's World Conception* (Spring Valley, NY: Anthroposophic Press, 1978, 3rd edition), GA2, p. 64.
71. Scheler, *Man's Place in Nature*, p. 36.
72. Novalis, *Hymnen an die Nacht*.
73. Steiner, *Philosophy of Freedom*.
74. Rudolf Steiner, *The Stages of Higher Knowledge*, 1931.
75. Johann Wolfgang von Goethe, *Goethe's Fairy Tale of the Green Snake and the Beautiful Lily* (New York: Steinerbooks, 1979), pp. 43–44.
76. Leeuw, *Der Mensch und die Religion*.

The Five Basic Books

THEOSOPHY, AN INTRODUCTION TO THE SUPERSENSIBLE KNOWLEDGE OF THE WORLD AND THE DESTINATION OF MAN by Rudolf Steiner. The book begins with a beautiful description of the primordial trichotomy: body, soul, and spirit. A discussion of reincarnation and karma follows. The third and longest chapter of the work (74 pages) presents, in a vast panorama, the seven regions of the soul world, the seven regions of the land of spirits, and the soul's journey after death through these worlds. A brief discussion of the path to higher knowledge is found in the fifth chapter.

Paper, $6.95 #155; Cloth, $10.95 #154

KNOWLEDGE OF THE HIGHER WORLDS AND ITS ATTAINMENT by Rudolf Steiner. Rudolf Steiner's fundamental work on the path to higher knowledge explains in detail the exercises and disciplines a student must pursue in order to attain a wakeful experience of supersensible realities. The path described here is a safe one which will not interfere with the student's ability to lead a normal outer life.

Paper, $6.95 #80

CHRISTIANITY AND OCCULT MYSTERIES OF ANTIQUITY by Rudolf Steiner. An introduction to esoteric Christianity which explores the ancient mythological wisdom of Egypt and Greece. The work shows how this wisdom underwent a tremendous transformation into a historical event in the mystery of Golgotha.

Paper, $7.95 #33

PHILOSOPHY OF FREEDOM by Rudolf Steiner. Steiner's most important philosophical work deals both with epistemology, the study of how man knows himself and the world, and with the issue of human freedom. In the first half of the book Steiner focuses on the activity of thinking in order to demonstrate the true nature of knowledge. There he shows the fallacy of the contemporary idea of thinking, pointing out that the prevailing belief in the limits to knowledge is a self-imposed limit that contradicts its own claim to truth. The possibility for freedom is taken up in the second half of the book. The issue is not political freedom, but something more subtle; freedom of the will. There are those who maintain that man's thoughts and actions are just as determined as a chemical reaction or a honey bee's behavior. Steiner points again to the activity of thinking, from which arises the possibility of free human action.

Paper, $5.50 #116

OCCULT SCIENCE, AN OUTLINE by Rudolf Steiner. This work of nearly 400 pages begins with a thorough discussion and definition of the term "occult" science. A description of the supersensible nature of man follows, along with a discussion of dreams, sleep, death, life between death and rebirth, and reincarnation. In the fourth chapter evolution is described from the perspective of initiation science. The fifth chapter characterizes the training a student must undertake to become an initiate. The sixth and seventh chapters consider the future evolution of the world and more detailed observations regarding supersensible realities.

Paper, $6.95 #113; Cloth, $10.95 #112

Rudolf Steiner and Anthroposophy

MAN AND WORLD IN THE LIGHT OF ANTHROPOSOPHY by Stewart C. Easton. A new and revised edition of Dr. Easton's survey of Rudolf Steiner's Anthroposophy. This comprehensive volume of over 500 pages complete with index is an excellent guide to Steiner's thought and works. Chapter titles include: "History and the Evolution of Human Consciousness," "Individual Spiritual Development and Human Freedom" and "Man and His Life on Earth and in the Spiritual Worlds; Reincarnation and Karma."

Cloth, $21.00 #353

RUDOLF STEINER: HERALD OF A NEW EPOCH by Stewart C. Easton. Dr. Easton's interest in Rudolf Steiner dates from 1934, when he first came into contact with Steiner's work, and he has been involved in anthroposophical activities in one way or another ever since. A historian by profession, Dr. Easton brings together in this book innumerable facts and details of Steiner's life that have been previously unavailable to English readers. The result is an outstanding portrait of a unique personality that will satisfy a long-felt need.

Paper, $10.95 #427

Other Books on the Esoteric Path of Spiritual Development

RUDOLF STEINER AND INITIATION by Paul Eugen Schiller. The author is a research scientist and a lifelong student of Steiner's works. In this book, translated from the German by Henry Barnes, Schiller presents a systematic discussion of Steiner's writings and lectures on the path of knowledge. Among the topics discussed are: "Fundamental Moods," "Development of the Six Attributes," "Sense Free Thinking, Feeling, and Willing," "Meditation," "Body Free Life of the Soul," "The Rosicrucian Path of Initiation," and "The Level of Inspirational Cognition."

Paper, $5.95 #418

THE CALENDAR OF THE SOUL by Rudolf Steiner. This is Steiner's famous collection of 52 verses, one for each week of the year. By following the verses through the year the soul gains a deeper insight and penetration into nature and the course of the seasons. The translation was made by Ruth and Hans Pusch.

Cloth, $7.95 #28

THE STAGES OF HIGHER KNOWLEDGE by Rudolf Steiner. In these four essays Steiner describes the experience of the three higher stages of consciousness: imagination, inspiration, and intuition which are experienced by the student, as he progresses on the path to knowledge, and by the initiate. The six exercises for the heart center are characterized as a means of protecting oneself from the "danger of mischief from hurtful forces" which would arise if one practiced meditation without the exercises.

Paper, $4.50 #146

THE INNER DEVELOPMENT OF MAN by Rudolf Steiner. This is a one lecture introduction to the nature of esoteric training or path of knowledge.

Booklet, $.95 #72

PRACTICAL TRAINING IN THOUGHT by Rudolf Steiner (Karlsruhe, 1909). This most popular pamphlet has been translated into many languages and published in innumerable editions. It is known throughout the world for its clear and concise directions for improving memory, thinking habits and powers of concentration.

Booklet, $1.50 #120

Steiner Education

The WALDORF or STEINER SCHOOL movement is one of the largest private school systems in the world. There are numerous Steiner schools in the United States with programs from kindergarten through high school. The Anthroposophic Press offers the following titles on this important approach to education:

THE RECOVERY OF MAN IN CHILDHOOD by A.C. Harwood. Probably the best introduction to Waldorf Education available. The work shows how the Waldorf approach to education is harmonized with the developmental phases of the child. Chapter titles include: "Threefold Relation of Body and Mind," "The Map of Childhood," "The First Seven Years," "The Small Child at Home and at School," "The Temperaments," "Adolesence," and "The High School." The work is highly recommended to the parents of prospective students and anyone wishing a clear understanding of the Waldorf School Approach.

Paper, $7.95 #411

THE WALDORF SCHOOL APPROACH TO HISTORY by Werner Glas, Ph.D. This important work is addressed to parents, teachers, and the general reader interested in education. It is based on ideas which have been put to the test in the classrooms of the rapidly expanding Waldorf School movement. Chapter titles include: "The History of Civilization," "In the Quest of the Images From Plutarch to Bryant," and "Seventh Grade and the Calyx of Modern Consciousness."

". . . a careful account of one aspect of the teaching that goes on in these Rudolf Steiner schools . . ." *(Commonweal)*

Paper, $6.95 #482

EDUCATING AS AN ART edited by Ekkehard Piening and Nick Lyons. An important collection of essays on different aspects of Rudolf Steiner education written by prominent American Steiner School teachers. The essays cover such topics as the meaning of discipline, fairy tales in the first grade, the teaching of Norse Myths, an arithmetic play for second grade, the teaching of history, and the future of knowledge. Many fine photos.

Paper, $7.95 #275

Order Form

If you enjoyed this book and would like another copy or if you want to order one of the books described on the preceding pages, please fill out the form below and mail it to us: Anthroposophic Press, 258 Hungry Hollow Road, Spring Valley, N.Y. 10977

Name _____

Address _____

City _____

State _____ Zip _____

Book #	Title	Price	Qty.	Amt.

Postage and Handling $1.75

Total Enclosed